# TO HER CREDIT

They'll tell you you're too loud—
that you need to wait your turn
and ask the right people for permission.

Do it anyway.

—Alexandria Ocasio-Cortez

# TO HER CREDIT

KAITLIN CULMO & EMILY McDERMOTT
*with art by* KEZIA GABRIELLA

UNION SQUARE & CO. and the distinctive Union Square & Co. logo are trademarks of Sterling Publishing Co., Inc.

Union Square & Co., LLC, is a subsidiary of Sterling Publishing Co., Inc.



ISBN 978-1-4549-4612-0 (hardcover)
ISBN 978-1-4549-4613-7 (e-book)

Library of Congress Control Number: 2022951256

For information about custom editions, special sales, and premium purchases, please contact specialsales@unionsquareandco.com.

Printed in Malaysia

2 4 6 8 10 9 7 5 3 1

unionsquareandco.com

Cover design by Melissa Farris
Cover art by Kezia Gabriella
Interior design by Christine Heun

# Contents

## Dropping the Bomb—on Science



## Women Don't Just Give Life: They Save It



## It Runs in the Family



## Coding New Realities



## Who Runs the World? Women.

# Introduction

THERE'S TRUTH TO THE CLICHÉD BREAKDOWN of the word "history": his story. The story of humankind has largely, until recently, been written solely by the men of the world, and the versions of the past recorded by the victors are the ones that are often still in textbooks.

Yet, throughout history, women have built many of the powerful institutions that define and control the world today—from the development of the degree-granting higher educational system to the discovery of nuclear energy to the invention of the technology behind Bluetooth and Wi-Fi. But many of these women have been overwritten in favor of *his*-tory. They have been forced to watch as the credit for their achievements has been awarded to men who had nothing to do with it, or their accomplishments were rejected and ignored until a man salvaged their forgotten work, raising it from the ashes—weeks, decades, even centuries later—and claiming it as his own.

Fortunately, such mis-accreditation has become less omnipresent in recent years, as women have been able to clarify and criticize purported narratives thanks to forces like social media and the internet. These technologies make transparency ever more accessible and false facts increasingly more difficult to perpetuate. But this was not always the case.

*To Her Credit* reclaims women's achievements that altered the world and society as we know it, but were ascribed to men throughout history. *To Her Credit* restores credit where credit is *actually* due.

It is important to note that the women featured in this book do not, by any means, comprise a comprehensive list. Rather, they offer examples of groundbreaking discoveries and pivotal moments across scientific, artistic, and humanistic fields. They are just a few examples showing that women have, despite what *his*tory says, built the backbone of society and spearheaded its development since antiquity.

The authors are also not discounting the contributions men have made to the building of the modern world, but rather correcting the collective narrative. Men have had their work stolen or miscredited too; however, the pattern throughout recorded history shows that this happens far more frequently to women.

Perhaps most importantly, it must be acknowledged that the list inherently skews toward Western, privileged women, due to both history's records and the authors' own limitations. Women throughout history were thought to be of such little consequence that those whose lives were recorded or whose letters were preserved—even if as a footnote—were often of relatively high social standing. There are undoubtedly countless women whose names, accomplishments, and lives were extraordinary but who have been lost to time. Lastly, the authors' own research capacities were also restricted to archives and stories that have been translated or written about in English. They know many more stories like these exist around the world in thousands of different languages.

# Women Writing History

*From humankind's first author to the first digital narrative, women have developed the concept of storytelling since the very beginning*



Imagine human civilization without written language—or without any writing at all. It's like imagining the world without the wheel. Writing, like the wheel, has played a fundamental role in shaping the physical infrastructure of human civilization, but it has also enhanced human culture as an art. Literature has taken on the role of conscience, shedding light on the inherent dangers of the day's intellectual or moral hubris through the simple act of storytelling.

Yet it took millions of years for letters and numbers to come into existence. And even once the first writing systems developed around 4000 BCE, it took thousands more years for written language to evolve into narrative storytelling. Despite this, there is a known historical account of writing and written storytelling: we know from where and whence language sprung forth from human mouth into hand; there is a first author and first work of literature, a first novelist and first novel.

What is often overlooked, however, is the fact that women are at the center of this story. Sometime between 2286 and 2251 BCE, a princess and high priestess of Mesopotamia—humankind's first civilization—became the first author in history. Three thousand years later, between 1001 and 1021 CE in what today is Kyoto, Japan, a Heian courtier invented the form of the novel. In 1818, Mary Shelley published a seminal book that gave the world the literary genre of science fiction, and in 1986, Judy Malloy programmed and wrote the first piece of fiction that lived entirely online, creating the first example of electronic fiction.

# Enheduanna

***ca.* 2286–2251 BCE**

OVER 4,300 YEARS AGO, PEOPLE LIVING IN the world's first civilization—ancient Sumer, part of the Mesopotamian empire—invented everything from wheeled carts, maps, and irrigation systems to astronomy, a number system, and the sixty-minute hour. But in the bustling Sumerian city of Ur (today, southern Iraq), the High Priestess of the Moon God Nanna was working on her own creation. She inscribed a collection of hymns on a soft clay tablet with a sharpened reed stylus, plucked from the watery riverbanks that flanked Sumer's growing cities. In doing so, she knew she was changing the course of human history. In the conclusion, she wrote: "The compiler of the tablets was En-hedu-ana. My king, something has been created that no one has created before."

That *something* was the concept of authored writing and, in turn, literature. Never before had anyone used cuneiform—mankind's first developed writing system, which had, at that point, existed for around 900 years—to convey stories, epics, hymns, or poems with the complexity that Enheduanna produced. Previously, cuneiform was used almost solely for tallying trade. Merchants and traders would communicate in cuneiform about their businesses, and priests and priestesses, who managed the stores of grain and animals in city temples, would use it to keep track of people's offerings. While early narrative writing and religious texts have been found that predate Enheduanna by a few hundred years, nothing compares to the scope of Enheduanna's work: she was the first person in history to incorporate the "I" into narrative writing; the first person to claim credit for their own work by signing their name; and the first person to fully develop characters with psychological dimension, emotion, and depth. In other words, Enheduanna was the world's first author.

Historians know that from 2286 to 2251 BCE, Enheduanna authored six long-form epic poems, and edited, compiled, and possibly wrote forty-two shorter lyric poems into a collection called *Temple Hymns*. Her most impressive surviving works are three epic poems revolving around heroic tales of Inanna, the goddess of love and war. These epic poems, *Inninsagurra, Ninmesarra,* and *Inninmehusa* (translated as *The Great-Hearted Mistress, The Exaltation of Inanna,* and *Goddess of the Fearsome Powers*), marked the first use of the pronoun "I" in a written form, and the first time a writer personally identified themselves within a narrative. Enheduanna passionately injects herself into the verses, like in her poem *The Great-Hearted Mistress*: "I am Enheduanna. I am the brilliant priestess of Nanna." Her strong authorial presence, found throughout *The Exaltation of Inanna*, is considered to be her greatest literary achievement, unmatched until the time of the Greek poetess Sappho, over sixteen hundred years later.

Enheduanna's poems also mark the first known example of an author describing their personal emotions in writing. Her works marked the beginning of how narrative writing could lead to self-reflection, how multiple perspectives could be introduced, and how emotions could be recorded. Enheduanna even recorded the first instance of sexual harassment while describing how a short-lived king made unwanted advances, "[wiping] his spit-soaked hand on Enheduanna's honey-sweet mouth." She also wrote erotically and passionately to her lover, "peg my vulva, my star-sketched horn of the dipper." Even more surprising, her temple was filled with cross-dressing and ambiguously gendered devotees, and through her poems, she wrote of how the goddess Inanna could smash mountains and turn "man into woman, woman into man."

By translating human emotion into words, not only did Enheduanna develop literary writing—which was largely centered on the sacred, creative powers of the divine feminine—she also found a way to unify the empire: her work became the first written propaganda. Her father had created the first empire by conquering every city-state in Mesopotamia, but the southern region resented his rule and often rebelled against him. Named the High Priestess of the largest southern city-state, Enheduanna compiled, edited, and possibly penned the *Temple Hymns*, an entirely new, politically motivated mythology that combined the northern and southern regions' distinct cultures into one new, shared religion.

Through her writing, Enheduanna quelled the social disquiet and culturally unified the world's first empire. Upon her death in 2251 BCE, her stories, hymns, and poems were continuously rewritten, performed, and copied for over a thousand years. After the dissolution of Mesopotamia, her work continued to influence writing and religion for centuries to come. Lines from her epic poems and hymns can even be found emerging through stories in the Hebrew Bible, as well as in the famous Homeric Hymns of ancient Greece and in the oral literature of ancient Indus Valley cultures.

But Enheduanna's name was lost in time. Her poems and hymns are indeed the world's first literary works and the first epic poems, making Enheduanna the first author. Today her body of work has been translated and her portrait is on display at the Penn Museum in Pittsburgh, but scholars have chosen to record literary history differently. *The Epic of Gilgamesh,* whose author is unknown, is widely credited as the world's first work of literature and epic poem, though it is dated more than 150 years after Enheduanna's death.

While *The Epic of Gilgamesh* was written over a century later than Enheduanna's work, it was rediscovered earlier. In 1835, British archaeologists came across an ancient library filled with clay tablets. For the next few decades, multiple scholars worked to decipher them; by 1872, what was uncovered of *The Epic of Gilgamesh* had been pieced together and translated. When the work was presented to the Society of Biblical Archaeology, British Prime Minister William Gladstone attended, and the discovery made front-page news across Europe and the United States.

Enheduanna's tablets, meanwhile, didn't resurface until 1927. But even when they did, they were greeted with little fanfare or recognition. The world was happy with its first epic poem and didn't need any new ones—especially, it seems, if they were written by a woman. The first scholarly article on Enheduanna didn't appear until 1958, and the first translations and book-length discussions on her work weren't published until ten years later. Even then, Enheduanna's name and humankind's earliest examples of epic poetry, as well as her other literary work, remained publicly unknown and academically unacclaimed.

Finally, at the turn of the 21st century, Betty De Shong Meador, a scholar at the University of California, Berkeley, began to unpack Enheduanna's history. Betty analyzed the theological, social, cultural, and political impacts Enheduanna had on the development of human civilization, and composed the first literary translations of her ancient body of work. But even now, with her work studied, translated, and published, prestigious publications, including *The New Yorker,* continue to cite *The Epic of Gilgamesh* as the world's first long poem.

# Murasaki Shikibu

***978–ca. 1014 CE***

BY THE 5TH CENTURY CE, THE WRITTEN language invented by the Chinese had found its way to Japan—a country which had, for centuries, admired all things developed by its neighbor. At the start of the first millennium, Japanese clans were dazzled by—and adopted as much as they could of—China's cosmopolitan riches and sophistication. Eventually, ruling-clan chieftains were replaced by emperors whose power was greatly influenced, if not modeled, after those in China. A new capital city, Heian-Kyo (today, Kyoto), was built at the turn of the 9th century, and women, who had once held powerful positions in Japan, lost their standings as Confucianism and Chinese Buddhism infiltrated Japan's societies. Chinese, now the official language of government, public life, and academic work—as well as Sino-Japanese, or *kambun*, a hybrid of Chinese and Japanese—was spoken *and written* only by men.

Fast-forward to the early 11th century and enter the Heian Period at its height. The upper class of Heian society was obsessed with beauty, ritual, and refinement. The duties of government officials included stylized dance performances, and imperial police were chosen for their looks as much as family connections. Poetry was regarded as the highest of all art forms; so while polygamy and promiscuity were norms, a poorly written poem could equate to social suicide.

During this time, women were forced to live behind silk screens and curtains, as they were not to be seen publicly; so they were accordingly also kept from scholarly spaces. Banned from learning Chinese, they spoke in Japanese and developed its first written form: *kana*, also called *hiragana*, or *onnade*, meaning "woman's hand." With *onnade*, women could write in their diaries, send notes to one another, and compose poems to recite in competitions among themselves. As their prose and poetry blossomed, so did another form of vernacular literature: fiction.

The Chinese considered fiction the crassest form of writing, and it had no place among circles of educated men. But among women, made-up tales flourished, inspired by daily rituals and a deep reverence for nature's beauty. One day, a miraculous piece of writing appeared in the Imperial City, captivating the attention of not only women but also men of the court. The words comprised the first few chapters of *Genji monogatari*, or *The Tale of Genji*, written by a courtier called Murasaki Shikibu.

Murasaki Shikibu (which, it should be noted, is a nickname; in Heian culture, it was a social faux pas to refer to someone by their given name, and Murasaki's real name remains unknown) was born in 978 CE in Heian-Kyo to a distant faction of the Fujiwara clan, a powerful political family that often intermarried with the royal family. In a society obsessed with status and style, this was a fortunate connection. Being a Fujiwara was not, however, Murasaki's only stroke of luck: her father, Fujiwara no Tametoki, secretly educated her alongside her brother, so she could speak and write Chinese. Her family connection, along with her growing reputation as a writer, were likely the reasons she was invited to become Empress Shōshi's lady-in-waiting at the Imperial Court in 1005 CE.



While a courtier, Murasaki wrote and released her novel chapter by chapter. Court men and women, even the Empress, anxiously awaited the release of each section, dying to know what trouble the fictional Prince Genji would find himself in next—almost like a modern-day reality show. Unfolding over fifty-four chapters (and in over 1,300 pages in the modern English translation), *The Tale of Genji* was a narrative unlike anything anyone had ever read—because it was the first narrative of its kind. With digressions, parallel plots, stories within stories, shifts of view, poetry, and a masterwork of prose, Murasaki describes the day-to-day happenings of real life in 11th-century Heian-kyo through Genji's fictional, but exceptionally familiar, world. She weaves together over four hundred characters from four generations, relaying the story of the prince's life and the thoughts of the women he encounters, as they reconcile life in a patriarchal society where walls are paper-thin and the only things to do are to navigate romances, gossip, and ruminate existentially.

*The Tale of Genji* was a massive literary feat. No prior written narrative had ever included such critical discourse between characters or presented such brilliant psychological interiority. It is as though the reader can hear the characters' thoughts, personally experiencing their motives and emotions. *Genji* was also unprecedented in its consistent literary themes: Murasaki wove concepts like the ephemeral beauty of nature, the fragility of love, and the struggle to find the meaning of life throughout the epic tale. When finally finished, *The Tale of Genji* was not only the world's first novel; it was also the first work of psychological literature.

In Eastern Asia, Murasaki was lauded as a cultural icon as soon as *The Tale of Genji* had been distributed throughout the empire. At the time of its release, copies were shipped throughout Japan's provinces, signaling a monumental shift in the way Japanese society regarded both fiction as a literary art and the accomplishments of women. Murasaki's diary, *Murasaki Shikibu Nikki*, also became well-regarded, as did her collection of 128 poems, *Poetic Memoirs*, which is believed to have been published in 1006 CE. After her death, somewhere between

1014 and 1025, *The Tale of Genji* continued to influence authorship, illustrations, theater, and other forms of art in Japan for more than a millennium.

In the Eastern regions of the world, the courtly women writers of the Heian Period are glorified to this day: in the year 2000, Murasaki was even honored with a place on Japanese yen banknotes. But in the West, the credit for Murasaki's revolutionary literary achievement has been given to someone else. Historians claim the Spanish writer Miguel de Cervantes's work *Don Quixote*, published in 1605 CE, as the first novel and the first example of psychological literature. But *Don Quixote* was published nearly six hundred years after Murasaki wrote *The Tale of Genji*. It's time the West looks toward the East, where the historic magnitude of Murasaki's *Tale of Genji* as a literary work—and as the world's first novel—has gone unmatched.

# Mary Shelley

***1797–1851***

AS A YOUNG GIRL IN 19TH-CENTURY LONDON, Mary Godwin grew up in an intellectually electrified household. Her father, the writer and philosopher William Godwin, was the first modern proponent of anarchism, and her mother, Mary Wollstonecraft, was a pioneering feminist thinker and writer at a time when writing as a profession was considered unsuitable for women. The Godwin-Wollstonecraft family was the epitome of counterculture in 1800s England.

The English values of the time can be summed up in one word: proper. Women should remain in their *proper* place—the home—and the *proper* gentleman was the intellectually superior breadwinner. Furthermore, everyone was expected to uphold *proper* societal values: modesty, piety, and duty. Young Mary, however, inherited her parents' rebellious spirits and did not abide by the repressive societal norms of her day; she ran away with the then-unknown poet Percy Bysshe Shelley when she was just sixteen years old.

While the Industrial Revolution pushed the country toward a new future in which the economy expanded and technology advanced, countercultures also emerged. Mary (now Mary Shelley), her husband Percy, and the famous poet Lord Byron, among others, began to shape a new movement against industrialization and their socially repressive society. They wanted no part in the rigid ideals of the day, wherein women were confined to the home. The young couple worried that humans were forgetting the sublimity and beauty of nature with each new technological innovation or scientific discovery. Through poetry and literature, they became purveyors of what is now called the Romantic movement.

In this context, Mary found herself at Lake Geneva in Switzerland in 1816, when she was eighteen years old, surrounded by other Romanticists. As part of a dare, she imagined and wrote a story about a mad scientist who brought a corpse back to life, inspired by the recent death of her newborn as well as a scientific exhibition where she watched electricity animate—and, perhaps, *revive*—a dead frog. This story soon became the first draft of *Frankenstein; Or, The Modern Prometheus*, the world's first science-fiction novel. But it was more than just the first instance of science fiction: it was a Gothic horror, a tragic romance, and a parable all sewn into one towering body.

Mary's name, however, was missing from the title page when *Frankenstein* was first published in 1818, and readers assumed that it had been written by her husband, who had by then achieved literary fame. Her name finally appeared on the cover of the revised edition, published thirteen years later in 1831, but throughout her life and into the future, she was continuously overshadowed by her husband's reputation. Her other writing went greatly neglected by the literary world. Sixty years later, in 1878, Edward Trelawny—a British biographer, novelist, and friend of Percy Shelley and Lord Byron—authored and published *Records of Shelley, Byron, and the Author.* In it, he questioned Mary's intellect and even her authorship of the book.

*Frankenstein,* although praised at the time of its publication, soon fell into the abyss and was largely forgotten until the 1930s, when it was adapted for the big screen and became a Hollywood hit. Writers such as Edgar Allan Poe and H. G. Wells, along with publisher Hugo Gernsback, are often incorrectly cited as the founders and men responsible for the popularization of the genre. Edgar was only nine years old when Mary published *Frankenstein*; Wells wasn't even born until forty-eight years later. Hugo didn't start publishing science-fiction stories until the 1920s, but even so, he's often called "The Father of Science Fiction." The Hugo Awards—the annual literary awards for the best works of science fiction and fantasy—are his namesake.

Aside from creating the genre of sci-fi, Mary also mothered the first post-apocalyptic novel when she wrote and published *The Last Man* (1826). A deeply personal work, *The Last Man* tells the story of the lone survivor of a worldwide plague, critiquing many aspects of Romanticism and featuring characters inspired by her husband and Lord Byron. Although it received poor reviews on publication, *The Last Man* was republished in the 20th century to increased critical appreciation, being a modern story with contemporary themes.

With works like *Frankenstein* and *The Last Man*, Mary not only produced thrillers, but also changed the literary possibilities of the future. At the time of *Frankenstein*'s writing, science fiction had neither a name nor any recognition as a separate form of literature. In fact, the term "scientist" did not yet even exist. By proposing scientifically based fantastic events, Mary's writing allowed fiction to move beyond realism and dependence upon ghost stories, miracles, and magic. Her reliance on science in storytelling was revolutionary.

# Judy Malloy

*1942–*

THE WORLD BEFORE EMAIL OR THE INTERNET might feel like ancient history, but Wi-Fi is only twenty-two years old, and not so long ago the computer weighed fifty tons. Within the millennia-spanning timeline of human history, today's digital world is incredibly new, beginning only four decades ago in Silicon Valley, California. Scientists, engineers, and tech pioneers congregated in the Bay Area in the 1980s, turning San Francisco into what remains the male-dominated epicenter of unprecedented high-tech discoveries and inventions, and ultimately the digital revolution. Alongside computer developments was the invention of new code languages. And as new forms of writing were digitized, so too was storytelling.

In 1986, the American poet and self-taught computer programmer Judy Malloy wrote and programmed the first digital storytelling platform and released a story called *Uncle Roger*. The necessity of printed stories was gone: on the computer, one could read and click through a narrative via the screen, and even re-read the story with different outcomes by selecting new pathways. It adapted the format of the *Choose Your Own Adventure* book series, and can be seen as a precursor to, more recently, the interactive Netflix film *Black Mirror: Bandersnatch*.

As an artist and writer, Judy had been interested in creating non-sequential narratives since 1977. At that point, without computers readily available, she started making experimental artist "books" with card catalogs. Each paper card in the catalog acted as an individual narrative unit; the entire catalog, or book, could be read and rearranged at will. As technology advanced, Judy was able to perfect her artistic vision. "Once in a while in a lifetime, everything comes together," Judy has written of her experience in 1986, the fateful year when *Uncle Roger* came to life. Nearly a decade after she began experimenting with non-sequential narratives, Judy had created not only the first piece of literature in a digital format now known as hyperfiction, or hypertext fiction, but the first work of a new genre: electronic literature.

"My vision was to create a computer-mediated novella in which the reader individually recreates a fictional environment by continually searching and retrieving narrative information," Judy said in 2014. Unlike a printed novel, *Uncle Roger* and other hypertext fiction stories are

Uncle
Roger
by
Judy Malloy

non-sequential. The author creates a fictional world populated by words and narratives, but the reader can enter at any place. Each reader's journey is individual, and the stories can be experienced in new ways time and time again.

At the time of its release, Judy's three-part narrative database appeared on Art Com Electronic Network and The WELL, two digital communities prior to the invention of the World Wide Web. It also set the standard for what the *Wall Street Journal* deemed "a future art form." This future art form was one of the first digital-native media; electronic literature excludes digitized printed material and has evolved along with technology. Stories like Judy's were meant to be experienced on a computer; today, this has morphed to include devices like smartphones and tablets, at times even requiring a touch-screen to be read.

Judy's ground-breaking contribution to the act of storytelling, however, is often overshadowed by American author and professor Michael Joyce's piece of hyperfiction, *afternoon, a story*, which he created in 1987 and officially released in 1990. Admittedly, *afternoon* had a few practical advantages: unlike *Uncle Roger*, it had an ISBN number, like printed books, so it could be sold and collected. It was also published at a time when, though still in its infancy, the Web could chronicle—and forever reflect—its successes. The critical praise for *Uncle Roger*, meanwhile, had been in print and wasn't converted to digital formats for decades to come; reviews of *Uncle Roger* and Judy's work at the time thus remained hidden in paper archives.

Yet there are also subjective reasons for Michael's success, the biggest of which was a 1992 *New York Times* article about hyperfiction titled "The End of Books." In it, the author discusses Michael at length, and *afternoon* is deemed "the granddaddy of full-length hypertext fictions." There is no mention of Judy or *Uncle Roger*, despite the fact that her story predates *afternoon* and helped pave the way for the future of electronic literature.

Although it might seem like this was just one omission in one article, the impact of the piece in the *New York Times* was field-defining. *afternoon* propelled Michael to fame within the industry, and receiving this title in such a well-respected and well-read publication cemented his position at the top of the genre—both in history and today. Since 1992, Judy's work has been exhibited, though she herself has only been a visiting fellow and lecturer at various universities. Michael, meanwhile, holds a tenured position at Vassar College. *afternoon* remains the most cited and most widely taught work of hypertext fiction and electronic literature, although Judy is the genre's real grande dame.

There's More to Art
than Meets the Eye

*Women artists have been at the forefronts of seismic shifts in creative fields, from the development of abstract painting to the conception of fictional films*



A movement that began at the turn of the 20th century, modernism was a revolution in every stratum of society in the early decades of the 1900s. In art, tradition was tossed out in one of the most radical style shifts European or American art history had ever seen. Representational, realist portraits and landscapes were replaced by whatever lawless form artists could conceive. And while cameras had existed since the early 1800s, the moving picture was an entirely new technology; in a matter of decades, films evolved into a completely new art form: cinema.

Kandinsky, Malevich, Mondrian, and Pollock: according to the Western art historical canon, these are the artists who pioneered Abstractionism and action painting—now considered tenets of modernist form. The Western art historical canon also bestows Solomon R. Guggenheim and Alfred H. Barr Jr. with the credit of establishing two of the most influential museums dedicated to modern and contemporary art. And Léon Gamount and Herbert Blaché are regarded by that same canon as two of the foundational figures of early cinema.

What the canon likes to neglect, however, are the facts that artists Janet Sobel and Hilma af Klint pioneered the styles adopted by Kandinsky, Malevich, Mondrian, and Pollock years earlier; that the Museum of Modern Art (MoMA) was actually founded by three women: Lillie P. Bliss, Abby Aldrich Rockefeller, and Mary Quinn Sullivan; and that it was Alice Guy Blaché who trained Herbert and made a name for Léon's production studio.

# Hilma af Klint

***1862–1944***

JUST AFTER THE TURN OF THE 20TH CENTURY, a woman engaged in spiritual practices began painting abstract scenes filled with vibrant colors, concentric circles, and dizzying spirals. The large canvases—some of which were nearly double her own height—were unlike anything previously made by a Western artist. She was, unbeknownst to those around her, pioneering a new artistic movement, one in which objects and figuration were replaced with nonobjective abstraction. But this woman, sequestered in her studio in Stockholm, Sweden, was ahead of her time: Hilma af Klint's work went unknown and unrecognized until the 1980s. Yet her male counterparts—painters like Vasily Kandinsky (1866–1944), Kazimir Malevich (1879–1935), and Piet Mondrian (1872–1944)—were lauded, years after Hilma had begun working, as the pioneers of Abstractionism.

Hilma was born just north of Stockholm in 1862 to Fredrik Victor af Klint and Mathilda Sontag, and she was their fourth of five children. Spiritualism was prevalent throughout the Victorian era, and, as was commonplace for the time, she attended her first séance—events where those in attendance communicate with the dead—at age seventeen. Then, following the sudden death of her sister Hermina in 1880 at age ten, Hilma became even more interested in spirituality and the occult; she turned toward Theosophy, a religious organization in which women were not only welcomed as members but also held senior positions. At the same time, Hilma became interested in art while attending the local Tekniska skolan (technical school), where she took classes in portrait painting.

Luckily for Hilma, women were permitted to study art in Sweden well before other European countries like Germany, Italy, and France. So she enrolled at the Royal Academy of Fine Arts in 1882 and graduated with honors in 1887. Upon graduation, she was awarded a studio, which she shared with two other artists, in central Stockholm. To earn money, she painted portraits and naturalist landscapes, two popular styles for women artists at the time, in addition to working as a draftsperson for a veterinary institute, making detailed drawings of animal surgeries.

While doing such work, however, Hilma continued regularly attending spiritual meetings, and she eventually began hosting weekly séances with four female friends, who went on to call themselves The Five. The Five's weekly meetings are what led to Hilma's leap into abstraction;

to the creation of what are now her most well-known works; to her career-defining paintings that earn her a place in art history.

During their séances, The Five would make contact with so-called "high masters" and copiously document their experiences in notebooks through automatic writings and drawings—a method that means writing and drawing without consciously guiding the movement of a pen on paper. These spiritual practices took place alongside scientific discoveries that pointed toward the previously unseen: the discovery of the X-ray, infrared light, and electromagnetic fields, for example. In the early 20th century, both religious and natural sciences were exploring the otherworldly. In other words, Hilma and The Five were neither alone in their quests nor seen as excessively eccentric in the public eye.

One day in 1904, a high master told Hilma during a séance that she was to make paintings on the astral plane, paintings that represented the immortal aspects of humankind. Thus, she took what had been automatic drawing and writing to the next level: automatic—or, in this case, abstract—painting.

Over the course of five years, Hilma created paintings based on this séance-based premonition. A series of 193 works was titled "The Paintings for the Temple," as they were, according to the high master, to be installed in a four-story temple with a spiral staircase at its center (the temple, however, was never built). She went on to paint many more abstract series, totaling almost 1,300 works. During her lifetime, though, Hilma showed these works to only a handful of people. Perhaps due in part to their reaction, she kept much of her abstract artistic activities secret and, fearing that the world would not yet accept or understand her work's abstraction, instructed her heir to hide her works for twenty years after her death in 1944.

When the crates were finally opened by her nephew in the late 1960s, the paintings and over twenty-six thousand pages of handwritten notes found within were astonishing works of abstraction, dated as early as 1906. Yet, by this time, male artists like Kandinsky, Malevich, and Mondrian had been established as the pioneers of abstraction, with their works dating back only to 1911.

It wasn't until forty-two years after her death—and twenty-two years after the end of her self-inflicted moratorium on showing her work—that Hilma's name resurfaced. In 1986, her work was included in the group exhibition "The Spiritual in Art: Abstract Painting, 1890–1985" at the Los Angeles County Museum of Art. But it took another twenty-seven years until she was the subject of a comprehensive survey exhibition in Europe ("Hilma af Klint: A Pioneer of Abstraction" in 2013 at the Moderna Museet in Stockholm) and another thirty-four years until she received a retrospective in the

United States ("Hilma af Klint: Paintings for the Future" in 2019 at the Solomon R. Guggenheim Museum in New York City).

Today, Hilma's name remains somewhat of a mystery, with her work continuing to be excluded from major historical exhibitions, including "Inventing Abstraction, 1910–1925" at MoMA in 2013. Art historians have, however, slowly begun to note Hilma's importance and her foundational, pioneering role in Abstractionism, including drawing parallels with the practices of her male counterparts that were also rooted in spirituality (Kandinsky, for example, was familiar with the religious movement of Theosophy and met its founder, Rudolf Steiner, as did Hilma). But where Kandinsky was a male, operating in a male-dominated industry and aided with the knowledge, as a trained lawyer, on how to sell himself, Hilma was a humble woman interested in producing art for the occult's sake rather than for personal gain. She was about something bigger than the individual ego: understanding human life in relation to an unending cosmos.

# Alice Guy Blaché

*1873–1968*

THE HISTORY OF HOLLYWOOD IS ONE OF male directors and male producers. The women in that story are the on-screen starlets, the "pretty faces." But before Hollywood became the epicenter of film, there was a burgeoning French cinema scene, émigrés of which founded the American industry as it came to be—and a woman named Alice Guy Blaché is at the center of this story. Until 2019, Alice was all but forgotten; however, since then she has become known as a pioneer of narrative fiction films, one of the first film directors, and one of the first owners of a wildly successful American film studio. But during her life and for decades after, her name had drifted into obscurity, just as the names of those she worked alongside—namely, her husband and the owner of a French production studio—were cemented in the history of cinema.

Born in 1873, Alice came of age at the same time cinematography began to emerge. She was raised between Chile, where her father owned bookstores; France, where she was born; and Switzerland, where she attended boarding school. When it came time to find a job, Alice trained as a stenographer and applied, in 1894, to work as a secretary for Léon Gaumont, one of many Frenchmen experimenting with the potential of moving images. Today, movies are associated with narrative, often fictional, storytelling; but at the beginning, Léon and others were focused on the mechanics of moving pictures as a way to document everyday life. They filmed workers leaving factories, crowds as they gathered for parades, and trains running along their tracks.

When Léon hired Alice, she observed these men observing daily life through film. Although she was fascinated by the technology just like them, she had a different idea: to make up a story and have friends act it out. "I thought that one might do better than these demonstration films," she wrote in her memoirs. Gathering her courage, she "proposed to Gaumont that [she] might write one or two little scenes and have a few friends perform in them."

Léon agreed, so long as she still fulfilled her secretarial work, and in 1896 Alice made *The Cabbage Fairy*. This short film became one of her greatest contributions to the history of cinema: it was not only Alice's first work of art, but one of the very first fictional films ever made. With its witty charm (the plot revolved around answering the question of where babies come from, the answer to which, at the time, was cabbage patches), Léon recognized the importance of what Alice had created. She was soon to abandon her office duties in favor of working as a location scout, casting director, costume designer, cinematographer, editor, writer, director, and producer for Gaumont Film Company.

One year later, in 1897, Alice was named head of production, a position she held for the next decade. During this time, on a professional level, she directed and produced over a thousand films. On a personal level, she met and married Herbert Blaché, a cameraman at Gaumont. She was forced to abandon her post at Gaumont in 1907 to move with Herbert to Ohio in the United States, where he had been promoted to head a Gaumont equipment franchise.

While Herbert attempted to expand the Gaumont empire, Alice established her own. By October 1910, a few years after she gave birth to her first child, Herbert's endeavors in Ohio had failed and they had moved to New York, where she founded her own company, Solax, and rented Gaumont's studio space for production. Alice's first film was released one month later, and she followed it by producing and directing one film every week for the next six months.

By mid-1911, Solax was producing two short films a week, and by 1912 the company was so successful that Alice decided to build her own studio in Fort Lee, New Jersey. The studio reportedly cost more than $100,000 (equivalent to about $3 million in 2022) to construct, but here the company continued its growth. Solax was soon producing three short films per week—at least half of which were written and directed by Alice, and for all of which she oversaw the production—and built a stable roster of movie stars with whom the studio worked.

But such unparalleled, uncomplicated success wasn't to last forever.



In 1913, Herbert's contract with Gaumont expired, so he joined Alice at Solax. After only three short months working alongside his wife, Herbert resigned and announced the formation of his own film company, Blaché Features. Blaché Features used Solax's new studio for filming and employed many actors who had become known for their appearances in Solax films. Alice, in addition to still producing films for Solax, also started directing movies for Blaché Features, alternating with her husband. Ultimately, the movies directed by both Alice and Herbert between 1913 and 1914 were sometimes branded Solax, sometimes Blaché Features. The line between the two companies became blurrier and blurrier. When Blaché Features's production outpaced that of Solax, Alice's company was altogether absorbed by her husband's.

What followed was a tumultuous period. On a personal level, Alice's legacy faded into the shadows with the demise of Solax, while around the same time their children contracted severe cases of the measles. Herbert sent Alice and the kids to North Carolina for recuperation, while he stayed in Fort Lee. During this time, he played the stock market and lost all of the family's savings—there was, after all, a national economic recession. Due in part to the recession and coal shortage caused by the outbreak of World War I, and in part to changing industry demands, Blaché Features also collapsed. There was a desire for longer films, and with them came a more centralized production and distribution system in Los Angeles. When Alice finally returned to New Jersey with healthy children in 1918, Herbert absconded with a young actress—who was also his mistress—to California, leaving his family penniless and Alice without a job.

Eventually, in the summer of 1919, Herbert brought Alice and the children to Los Angeles. They lived in separate houses, and Alice's only work was to occasionally assist Herbert, who had begun directing Hollywood hits. Alice accepted that their marriage was over and, in 1922, moved back to France with her children.

As Herbert's career continued to grow and he went on directing films in Hollywood, Alice never made another movie again. From 1922 until 1927, she sought work in the French film industry, but to no avail. In 1927, she even returned to the United States to retrieve copies of her films to help her secure work in France, only to find that none of them existed anymore—not even those that she had deposited and copyrighted at the Library of Congress. Following this disheartening discovery, alongside the end of the silent film era in 1929, Alice became financially dependent on her children, a position in which she would remain until her death in 1968.

Adding salt to the wound, when Léon Gaumont published a history of the Gaumont Film Company in 1930, he included neither Alice's name nor her pioneering work for the company. When Herbert had founded Blaché Features, he hadn't mentioned his wife by name in any of the surrounding press materials either. But instead of succumbing to disappointment or resentment, Alice realized the only way she'd be remembered was if she fought for it herself—and so she did.

From 1947 until 1952, Alice poured her energy and focus into writing her own memoirs, crafting her own filmography, and once again searching for her films. During this period, she began corresponding with Louis Gaumont, Léon's son, who, in 1954, gave a speech in Paris on "Madame Alice Guy Blaché, the First Woman Filmmaker," stating that she had been "unjustly forgotten." Although this inserted her legacy into the canon and she received a few local honors following his speech, her name largely remained in the shadows and her memoirs were published only posthumously in French in 1976. Herbert and Léon, meanwhile, became staples of the history of film, with their names appearing on college syllabi and in history books around the world. Alice's name would occasionally appear as a footnote to theirs, but it wasn't until 2019, when Pamela B. Green released a feature-length documentary (narrated by Jodie Foster and featuring a number of never-before-seen films, artifacts, and documents rescued from Alice's family's storage), that Alice began to receive the long-overdue attention and credit she deserves: that of being a revolutionary, critical pioneer of the film industry as we know it.

MOMA

# Lillie P. Bliss, Abby Aldrich Rockefeller, and Mary Quinn Sullivan

***1929***

MANY OF THE MOST RENOWNED MUSEUMS in New York City today, including the Whitney Museum of American Art, the Solomon R. Guggenheim Museum, and the Museum of Modern Art, were founded less than a century ago, and for a reason: few moments in European or American history prior to the turn of the 20th century saw such radical shifts in art. Artists were embracing new techniques, veering away from traditionally accepted forms of representational, realist portraits and landscapes. Many museums, however, were slow to accept these new perspectives as "art." So, when MoMA opened its doors in 1929—with the Whitney (1931) and Guggenheim (1939) soon to follow—it was revolutionary.

MoMA was conceived one day in 1928 over lunch, when three women—Lillie P. Bliss, Abby Aldrich Rockefeller, and Mary Quinn Sullivan—had the idea to found a museum in New York dedicated to exhibiting modern art. There were smaller galleries showcasing new, contemporary works, but to create an institution dedicated to artistic movements happening in the present moment, rather than historic presentations, was unheard of. As MoMA's first brochure stated, "New York alone, among the great capitals of the world, lacks a public gallery where the works of the founders and masters of the modern schools can be seen." So Lillie, Abby, and Mary committed to building the very first institution of its kind: a museum exclusively dedicated to the exhibition of modern art.

These "daring ladies," as they were socially known, set to work, and in November 1929 MoMA opened in a rented space in a building on the corner of Fifth Avenue and 57th Street, only a few blocks from where the museum stands today. The opening exhibition, "Cézanne, Gauguin, Seurat, Van Gogh," drew crowds. Over forty-seven thousand people visited during its one-month run, and critics lauded the display. But those same critics also praised Alfred H. Barr Jr. for his visionary direction of the museum—not the three women who had dedicated their fortunes, as well as intellectual efforts, to its founding.

Lillie, Abby, and Mary were women of high social standing: Lillie was born in 1864 and was heir to her father's textile empire; Abby, born in 1874, married Standard Oil heir John D. Rockefeller Jr., whose father became America's first billionaire; and Mary, born in 1877, was trained in art education and wed to a prominent lawyer. They each collected art personally, acquiring impressive ranges of works by now-iconic modern artists including Paul Cézanne, Henri Matisse, Pablo Picasso, Pierre-August Renoir, and Georges Seurat, among many others. It was their social privileges that afforded them the funds and connections to found their new museum. Plus, when Lillie died in 1931, only two years after the museum opened, she bequeathed more than 150 paintings, prints, and drawings to the museum; these works became the nucleus of its collection, and many still hang in MoMA's galleries today. Over the years, Abby also donated nearly two thousand invaluable works of art to the collection, in addition to thousands of dollars to be used for acquisitions.



But when Lillie, Abby, and Mary founded their new museum and invited industrialist Anson Conger Goodyear to become president, he invited two more men, Paul J. Sachs and Frank Crowninshield, to join him as founding trustees. He then appointed a young art historian, Alfred H. Barr Jr., as the director. With these appointments, the women's own relationships to one another and their roles within their own institution were soon largely overwritten; as an archivist at the Rockefeller Archive Center poignantly said around 2015, relationships between women were not considered worth archiving at the time. So, even as MoMA rose to worldwide renown, no one wrote about or even took a photo of the three women together, as one would expect of the cofounders of one of the world's most famous museums.

Instead, Alfred's name rose to fame—so much so that he is often cited as the museum's founder. Books have been written about MoMA's history and "the biography of its founder Alfred Barr." One such book, written by Sybil Kantor and published in 2003 by the MIT Press, is even titled *Alfred H. Barr, Jr. and the Intellectual Origins of the Museum of Modern Art*, with the synopsis explaining how the author traces the rise of modern art in America and the story of "the man responsible for its triumph."

Alfred did indeed have a pioneering vision for the museum, and he established important programs that remain in place today, including MoMA's representation of all types of art, from painting to photography to architecture to film. However, his legacy exists only due to the initial brainchild of three groundbreaking, boundary-pushing women. And although Lillie, Abby, and Mary all remained members of the board of trustees until they died or actively resigned, it's unclear exactly what their roles entailed once Alfred became the director: historians did not write about the women; they wrote about Alfred.

Parallel to the female founders of the museum being written out of its history for much of the last century, the men who took charge of the museum placed a primary focus on male artists, too. In the 1930s, only 8 percent of the artists in the museum's exhibitions were women (by the 1980s, this number had risen only to 14 percent), and for almost an entire decade following its opening, MoMA did not hold a single one-woman exhibition. Eventually it did—but even still, only 102 of the 2,052 exhibitions MoMA held between 1929 and 2010 were focused specifically on women.

Over the course of the last century, Lillie, Abby, and Mary's museum has become synonymous with world-class presentations of new movements in artistic activity and creativity; a mirror to our modern world. However, the legacies of these pioneering women—as well as the works of countless women artists—have largely been remembered only when nestled between works by and praise for their male peers.

# Janet Sobel

***1893–1968***

ONE DAY IN 1938, A FORTY-FIVE-YEAR-OLD woman began experimenting with her son's painting supplies in her apartment in Brighton Beach, Brooklyn, New York City. At first, she painted dreamlike forms floating in enchanted landscapes. But soon, following her gut, she abandoned such figurative inclinations. She threw and poured paint on unstretched canvases laid out on the ground. She used glass pipettes to control the pigment as it fell, splashing. She even used a vacuum cleaner to move enamel around, stretching it from thick splatters into thin gossamers, leaving no brushstrokes behind. She gave each and every part of the canvas equal attention, creating the first of what later would be deemed an "allover" surface with a "drip painting" technique—two hallmarks of the American Abstract Expressionist movement, especially the New York school of the 1940s.

The name of the woman behind this development, however, would soon be lost to her peers of the opposite sex: Janet Sobel became a footnote, used solely to frame the work of male artists, namely Jackson Pollock.

Janet was born as Jennie Lechovsky in a shtetl near Ekaterinoslav in Russia (now the town of Dnipro in Ukraine) in 1893. When her father was killed in a Russian pogrom, the family decided to emigrate to the United States. Upon landing at Ellis Island in 1908, she changed her name to Janet and settled with her mother and siblings in the Brooklyn neighborhood of Brighton Beach. Two years later, she married Max Sobel, who also immigrated to the US from Ukraine, and the couple had five children.

Janet had never expressed much of an interest in art or studied it herself (later, she even admitted that she didn't visit museums much, given her responsibilities as a wife and mother). Sol, however—one of her sons—enrolled at the prestigious Art Students League in the 1930s. Legend has it that one fateful evening, Janet criticized one of her son's paintings. He threatened to quit his studies at the nonprofit school in Manhattan, which counted renowned artists like Norman Rockwell, Georgia O'Keeffe, and Mark Rothko as alumni; he threw down his brush and told his mother to take up painting herself—and she did.

While her son had been attending art school, she had already started experimenting on various surfaces, including pieces of mail and scraps of cardboard. But this exchange with Sol allegedly pushed her to the next level, and Janet began to work on canvas. Both surprised and impressed by his mother's work, Sol sent letters introducing her paintings to prominent artists and philosophers of the time, including Max Ernst, André Breton, John Dewey, and Sidney Janis. The latter included her work in a group exhibition in Chicago in 1943. She had her first solo exhibition at Puma Gallery in New York in 1944.

The group show in Chicago, however, was titled "American Primitive Painting of Four Centuries," reflecting the space to which most of the art community was relegating her work: the *outside*, the *primitive*. She was, as critics repeatedly stated, not only untrained as an artist but also a mother, a grandmother, and a housewife. For the critics and art world of the 1940s, these latter roles overshadowed her talents as a creator. Her work was seen positively, but only through the lens of the primitive housewife.

Surrealist artists, like Max and André, who had also immigrated to New York from Europe as refugees during World War II, recognized Janet's astounding talents and separated them from her domestic roles. They would visit Janet at home, where they'd look at her work and have dinner together. In turn, Max eventually introduced her work to his wife, the influential art collector and dealer Peggy Guggenheim.

Peggy proved an invaluable key to unlocking Janet's career as an artist: she included Janet's work in a group show, "The Women," at her gallery, which was named The Art of This Century, in 1945; the following year, her work was again shown at the gallery in a solo exhibition. Some critics lauded the exhibition. *Art News*, for example, contrasted her earlier "primitive" work with what they now deemed "highly sophisticated abstractions." But others wouldn't let the clichés go. The local paper, *The Brooklyn Eagle*, titled one article "Critics Acclaim Boro [short for Borough] Grandmother as Top Flight Surrealist Painter." She might've been "top flight," but she was still a local grandmother.

Shortly thereafter, in 1947, Janet and her husband moved to Plainfield, New Jersey, because he wanted to be closer to his work. Now physically distant from the New York art scene and having also developed an allergy to an ingredient in paint, her production was limited, and the burst of attention she had garnered in the preceding three years began to dwindle. Moreover, Peggy decided around the same time to relocate to Europe and to shutter the doors of her gallery. Despite Sidney's 1946 assertion in the *Brooklyn Eagle* that "Janet Sobel will [. . .] be known as one of the important surrealist artists in this country," by 1948 her name and work had vanished from the art world entirely.

It wasn't until 1961, only seven years before Janet's death, that her name resurfaced. The influential and authoritative art critic Clement Greenberg was chronicling the work of his dear friend, the artist Jackson Pollock, who, just like Janet, dripped enamel paint onto massive, unprimed, unstretched canvases laid on the ground. By the 1960s, Jackson was—and still is—known as one of the most important artists of the century and a founder of Abstract Expressionism, due in large part to what is ascribed to be his development of the "allover" and "drip" painting techniques. But in a collection of his essays published in 1961, Clement updated one pivotal piece of writing, "American Type Painting," first published in 1955. The updated essay admitted that he and Jackson had not only noticed Janet's work in the group exhibition in 1944, but that they had "admired [the] pictures rather furtively." He continued, writing: "It was the first really 'all over' one [painting] that I had ever seen," and that "Pollock admitted that these pictures had made an impression on him." Along with these accolades, however, Clement was adamant in pointing out that Janet "was, and still is, a housewife living in Brooklyn," as well as calling her a "'primitive' painter." Her name was even misspelled as Janet "Sobol."

Janet's status as a "primitive" painter made it easy for men to write her out of art history. She could be relegated to the roles of an outsider, a housewife, a mother, and a grandmother, who just happened to interlope for a few years in New York's art scene. But Clement's revised essay makes the truth clear to those reading with a critical eye: Janet Sobel deserves to be much more than a footnote. Though she died in obscurity in 1968, she was in fact the first known artist ever to create allover and drip paintings; not, as history has recorded, Jackson Pollock—the artist who she inspired, who ultimately made allover and drip paintings an iconic staple of the New York school and Abstract Expressionism.

Music to a
Woman's Ears

*From classical compositions to contemporary rock and roll, women have paved the way for many of music's male icons*



Music has, in some way, shape, or form, existed since the beginning of human history. Before the concept of writing was developed, music was improvised and created on the spot. But as written language began to develop in ancient Chinese, Egyptian, Greek, Indian, Mesopotamian, and Middle Eastern societies, so too did musical notation. And when the printing press was invented in the 15th century, sheet music could be more easily disseminated. With this, cohesive musical styles began to develop across different cultures.

In the West, this gave rise to the European Baroque period, during which music became tonal rather than modal. In other words, it was composed according to a richer and more complex system than previously, and it also led to the world's first operas. But hot on Baroque's heels came what is now universally recognized as the Classical period in music. In essence, Classical composers of the 18th and 19th centuries let their music speak for itself. Instead of using instruments to simply accompany operatic singing, as was often the case in the Baroque period, Classical music put the sounds of the instruments in focus.

Meanwhile, genres like pop music and rock and roll only started to develop at the turn of the 20th century as technology advanced: instruments became more accessible; the radio allowed music to easily be heard in every home. And with this changing media landscape, the world's first "pop stars" emerged.

Instantly recognizable names exist from nearly every stage of the modern history of music. An exemplary Baroque figure is Johann Sebastian Bach. Classical legends include Wolfgang Amadeus Mozart and Franz Joseph Haydn. Felix Mendelssohn was one of many stars of the next period, the Romantic. And when recalling the stars of early rock and roll, names like Elvis Presley and Chuck Berry likely come to mind.



But behind Wolfgang, Felix, Elvis, and Chuck were female pioneers. Wolfgang's sister Maria Anna was as talented as her brother, if not more so. Felix's sister Fanny composed many pieces that up until recently had been considered "his" work. The sounds and personas supposedly first embodied by Elvis and Chuck were actually developed by Sister Rosetta Tharpe. And the song that put Elvis at the top of the *Billboard* charts for eleven straight weeks and skyrocketed him to worldwide fame wasn't even his; it was written for Willie Mae—aka Big Mama—Thornton.

# Maria Anna Mozart

*1751–1829*

"VIRTUOSIC," "A PRODIGY," "GENIUS." THESE were the words used in the 1760s to describe the musical gifts of Mozart—Maria Anna Mozart, that is. Unlike her younger brother, Wolfgang Amadeus, however, Maria Anna's name and musical genius has been all but lost to history.

Maria Anna, nicknamed Nannerl, was born in Salzburg, Austria, in 1751, five years before her brother. Music was an integral part of her life from a young age, as her father, Leopold, was a composer, conductor, and accomplished violin player. By the age of seven, Maria Anna had learned to play the harpsichord, with her three-year-old brother sitting by her side. Within a few years, Wolfgang began attempting to play sections from his sister's music book. One day before his fifth birthday, Wolfgang learned to play a minuet and trio "in half an hour, at half-past nine at night on the 26th of January 1761," Leopold jotted down in one of Nannerl's music books. To their father's surprise, the family had not one but two child prodigies.

From that moment on, Leopold musically trained both his children and gathered the funds to showcase their talents across Europe. The family was neither wealthy nor noble, but he saw his children's potential to awe audiences. Few young adults could perform the most advanced sonatas and concertos by great composers on the harpsichord and fortepiano with precision, lightness, and poise—let alone children aged eleven and six.

In 1762, the family embarked on their first tour through western and central Europe, and its success led to a second, grander tour the following year, during which they stopped in eighty-eight cities. Maria Anna and Wolfgang played side by side in the homes of nobility and in grand halls for general audiences, performing in front of thousands of people. They became known as the Mozart *wunderkinder*. Following a performance in Munich, Germany, in 1762, Count Karl von Zinzendorf wrote in his diary that the "little fellow plays marvelously," and that "his sister's playing is masterly." The same year, Leopold wrote to a friend back in Salzburg: "Little Nannerl . . . plays with such skill that the world talks of her and marvels at her."

When on tour in 1764, Leopold fell ill during a stop outside of London. The family stayed put for his recovery, and during this time the children recorded what became known as Wolfgang Amadeus Mozart's first symphony, K. 16. What is fact is that Maria Anna, with a quill pen and parchment, wrote the notes down. What is murkier, however, is how the symphony came to be: only a fly on the wall would be able to say whether Maria Anna merely wrote down what Wolfgang was playing, or if the two collaborated on its composition. Some historians argue the former, while others stand by the latter. As Noel Zahler, director of the School of Music at Carnegie Mellon University, once remarked: "They probably had lots of discussion about what he was doing. I'll bet she . . . suggested some things for the horns and for other parts of the composition as well."

The family continued touring together, with Maria Anna and Wolfgang reveling in their shared musical abilities. Their bond was tight, but as time passed, their father began to focus his energies on only one child—and when he decided it was time to tour again in 1769, only one child was to go on the road with him: Wolfgang.

Maria Anna was, by then, eighteen years old, the age at which she became eligible to marry. Society at the time permitted women to compose and perform music, but only those of noble descent, for women had to play their music for free. Given the Mozart family's middle-class standing, as soon as Maria Anna crossed the threshold from innocent child to young woman, she would have either been bankrupted by the pursuit of music or considered a prostitute if she had tried to earn a living with it. So, to maintain a respectable reputation, she was relegated to the family's home while her brother and father were off touring the continent.

This didn't stop her love of music, though. Maria Anna continued to correspond with Wolfgang, who sent her sheet music to study so the siblings could play together upon his return. She even composed her own songs and sent them to him. In one letter dated July 7, 1770, Wolfgang remarked, "I am amazed! I had no idea you were capable of composing in such a gracious way. In a word, your Lied is beautiful. I beg you, try to do these things more often."

But this piece of music has never been found. In fact, no piece of music written by or collaboratively produced with Maria Anna has ever surfaced.

In 1781, a family dispute ruptured the siblings' relationship. Wolfgang defied their father's wishes and left Salzburg in pursuit of greater fame and fortune, while Maria Anna sided with their father and remained at home. She eventually then settled into family life, marrying in 1783. From previous marriages, her husband had five children, for whom she was now responsible, and together the pair had three more children of their own (although one, Maria, only survived for about a year).

For the remainder of her life, Maria Anna spent her time caring for her father, her husband, and their children. Following her brother's early death in 1791, she met his widow, Constanze. Together, they sifted through papers and letters that had been exchanged among the family members until he left in 1781, and used them to write a biography of Wolfgang. Maria Anna herself never received such treatment.

Today, the name Wolfgang Amadeus Mozart is synonymous with musical genius, while Maria Anna—Wolfgang's biggest supporter, inspiration, and perhaps even collaborator—is buried in the footnotes. The definitive 1984 Hollywood biopic *Amadeus* doesn't even mention the fact that Wolfgang had a sister, let alone give her a role in the narrative. Nannerl's existence might live on in portraits, letters, and early reviews of their duets, yet her music that was praised throughout Europe has never been found.

# Fanny Mendelssohn

***1805–1847***

FROM ROUGHLY 1780 TO 1830, THE ROMANTIC period developed throughout Europe, coinciding with what's known as the Victorian Era in England. The Romantics emphasized individual self-expression, which grew out of the ideas of individualism that came about during the Age of Enlightenment; yet they rejected the Enlightenment's emphasis on logic and rationality. They rebelled against constraints and rules concerning Classical music as well as against the hallmarks of the Industrial Revolution, including mechanization, mass production, and urbanization. Instead, the Romantics were focused on achieving an idealized, natural state of being.

During this time, Classical musicians experimented and broke previously established musical "rules." They developed compositions inspired by natural landscapes and literature, compositions created according to personal feelings. In other words, they twisted rules and regulations to create emotional works of sonic art that pushed boundaries that had been established by their predecessors like Mozart and Haydn. This shift toward emotionality instead of rigor began with Ludwig van Beethoven's novel notions at the turn of the century, and continued with the Romantics.

One of the most well-known compositions from this era is now often heard as brides walk down the aisle. The tune, referred to as the "Wedding March," was written by the German composer Felix Mendelssohn and is from his concert overture for Shakespeare's play *A Midsummer Night's Dream*. Felix was undoubtedly a genius; he was likened to a second Mozart, had his first *Singspiel* (similar to an opera) performed by a professional orchestra and singers on his twelfth birthday, and wrote the overture to *A Midsummer Night's Dream* as a teenager. While this famous composition is without question Felix's work, a murkier truth lies behind a large part of the identity of this great, individual musician that history remembers. In reality, Felix composed and collaborated with another musical prodigy and genius: his sister, Fanny. But he published and performed many of their shared works under his own name.

Both Fanny and Felix grew up in the early 1800s among Germany's elite, surrounded by artists and intellectuals. In their early years, the two children were musically educated by their parents. Both Fanny and Felix, four years his sister's junior, received their first piano lessons from their mother, whose own teacher

had studied under Johann Sebastian Bach. As they grew older, they continued to practice piano, as well as study other instruments, with famous teachers, even moving for a time to Paris to receive advanced instruction. In one letter in 1831, the siblings' teacher, Carl Friedrich Zelter, wrote to the famous poet Johann Wolfgang von Goethe that "She plays like a man"—the highest compliment a woman could receive at the time. In fact, the day after Fanny was born on November 14, 1805, in Hamburg, Germany, her father had even written a letter to his mother-in-law, reporting a prophetic observation: their newborn daughter had "Bach-fugal fingers."

However, Fanny was limited by the prevailing attitudes of the time toward women. Both Felix and Fanny, especially because of their aristocratic positions, adhered to 19th-century bourgeois gender roles. So, although Fanny was, by all accounts, as talented as her brother if not more so, their father began limiting the amount of music in his daughter's life by 1820. In a letter to his daughter, he wrote, "Music will perhaps become Felix's profession, while for you it can and must be only an ornament, never the root of your being and doing."

Fanny played at her family's fortnightly Sunday musicals at their home, but she was not allowed to give public concerts, as her brother began doing to great acclaim in his teens. She also composed many choral and piano pieces, but was never allowed to publish them.

That didn't stop Felix from publishing at least six of Fanny's works under his own name. Though it wasn't generally known at the time, one music critic wrote: "Three of the best [of Felix's twelve published songs] are by his sister, a young lady of great talents and accomplishments."

One of Fanny's songs, "Italien," which had been published under her brother's name, became a favorite of Queen Victoria, who even then sang it for Felix in 1842. Felix wrote in a letter: "It was really charming . . . then I was obliged to confess that Fanny had written the song (which I found very hard, but pride must have a fall), and beg her to sing one of mine also."

Felix relied heavily on Fanny in his own compositions. He consulted her constantly on his new works, and after she arranged private performances of his pieces before their public debuts, she helped him make revisions. Countless letters indicate the amount of time they spent together, playing, practicing, and exchanging. At one point Fanny wrote: "He never writes down a thought before submitting it to my judgment. For instance, I have known his operas by heart before a note was written."

Although for most of her forty-one years she practiced her art very privately among a circle of family and friends, beginning in 1831 Fanny started to host a weekly musical salon at her Berlin home. Invitations to her events were highly sought after, and it was only at these coveted gatherings that Fanny was able to perform her music for an audience—yet it was still only within her own abode. She programmed each concert, played the piano, and conducted and composed music, while her husband worked on the visual aspects of the performances.

Beyond these salons, there are only three documented performances in which Fanny played publicly: all of them were charity concerts and none of them featured her own music. Rather, at each of these three events, she played her brother's compositions.



Since the fall of the Berlin Wall in 1989, when archives in the former East Germany became available to researchers, the full scope of Fanny's accomplishments has been slowly starting to emerge. We now know that Fanny wrote over 460 compositions during her lifetime, and while a handful were published under her brother's name, most were never officially published at all. With the support and encouragement of her husband, the well-known artist William Hensel, though, she published a collection of songs under her own name in 1846, a year before she died of a stroke while conducting a rehearsal of her brother's *Walpurgisnacht*.

While largely removed from public view for the majority of her life, Fanny was nonetheless driven to compose and remained dedicated to her art, which she practiced faithfully for nearly thirty years. Composition was her constant companion, evidenced by her prolific output, including lieder, chamber, choral, and orchestral works. Though she received little public recognition during her life, her name was not completely lost to history, due in large part to her family's upper-class status and her brother's fame. Nevertheless, her work wasn't properly attributed to her until recent decades, when music historians and musicians began making it a point to highlight Fanny's contribution to Felix's legacy—making it clear that Fanny was a genius in her own right—and, indeed, many of Felix's supposed works were actually hers.

# Rosetta Nubin, aka Sister Rosetta Tharpe

*1915–1973*

ROSETTA NUBIN WAS BORN IN 1915 INTO A field-working, musically oriented family on a farm in Cotton Plant, Arkansas. Despite the difficulties imposed by being a Black woman living in the segregated Jim Crow South—a violent, oppressive world for Black folk, where social standards were defined by and for whites—Rosetta had joined her mother singing at their church, the African American Pentecostal Church of God in Christ, or COGIC, by the age of four.

In COGIC services, congregants shouted and moved to express their faith—the exact opposite of the mainstream (and white) Protestant churches of early 20th-century America, which prohibited any sounds that might incite the body to move. While Protestants stood still and solemnly sang, COGIC worshippers incorporated elements of blues, work songs, and ragtime into their music; they created a hybrid style fusing the spirituals of enslaved people with traditional hymns. At churches like Rosetta's, enlivened singing and dancing cemented the role of one's body as an instrument of God.

As Rosetta grew up, she and her mother took COGIC's spirit and ran with it. COGIC churches had sprung up around the United States, and in 1921, at the behest of a COGIC program that—rare for the time—encouraged women to work, Rosetta's mother became a preacher. Six-year-old Rosetta and her mother moved to Chicago, where Ms. Nubin gave sermons at COGIC's Robert Temple Fortieth Street Church.

Rosetta and her mother were just two of millions of African Americans to migrate north during the early 20th century, fleeing racial violence and discrimination in the South. Luckily for Rosetta, she and her mother would come to find more than just economic and social opportunity at Fortieth Street. The church was a gospel hub in the midst of the Chicago Black Renaissance, the creative movement of African American writers, artists, and musicians that flourished in the early decades of the 1900s on the city's South Side. Musically, the Great Northward Migration brought with it the post-slavery blues and church gospel of the South, which mixed with the culture of jazz and big band. The result: a music renaissance booming out of Chicago. Rosetta and her mother had moved into the very heart of gospel music's rising.

While her mother preached, it was Rosetta herself who became the star of the Sunday services, playing an adult-size electric guitar and performing gospel with such skill that she was called the "singing and guitar-playing miracle." The electric guitar was a new, intimidating invention, and Rosetta, even at her young age, was one of the first to embrace it. Word quickly spread, and people from outside the church started attending services—not for prayer, but to watch the little prodigy. She and her mother soon began traveling so Rosetta could perform at COGIC conventions and churches around the country, and they wouldn't stop until Rosetta became the first gospel singer to sign with a major record label. In 1938, she signed with Decca Records, and her recording of "Rock Me" was the first gospel record to sell over a million copies.

By 1938, Rosetta had married and divorced her first of three husbands, whose surname, Tharpe, she adapted as her lifelong stage name. She also began collaborating with Marie Knight, another gospel singer and pianist, with whom she had both a professional and intimate relationship—an "open secret" in the gospel world. Rosetta could sing and hold strenuous notes and sexy growls; she swayed, moved, and rocked onstage. She not only played the electric guitar: she gave the instrument a voice of its own.

Yet Rosetta's way with the guitar was not purely of her own accord. She was deeply inspired by Arizona Juanita Dranes, a musician and singer who had also made a name for herself within the Black COGIC community at a young age. A spirited pianist, Arizona, who had become blind after a serious bout of the flu as a child, invented the high-energy gospel beat and brought that sound, by the 1920s, into the Pentecostal church, within which Rosetta was raised. Arizona used the piano as a distinct voice, and her pioneering spirit and techniques are reflected in the ways Rosetta plucked single guitar strings rather than strumming chords and slid her fingers along the strings. Much like Arizona and the piano, Rosetta made the guitar talk in ways never before heard.

The more music Sister Rosetta Tharpe wrote and recorded, the more the rock and roll sound took shape. Rosetta's tracks were infused with upbeat gospel and blues, and meshed big-band jazz with brilliant solos on the electric guitar. In 1938, Rosetta gave a groundbreaking performance at New York City's Cotton Club, the only integrated nightclub in the metropolis. The legendary show marked the first time gospel music was taken outside church walls—the musical fruits of African American religious labor entered the secular world through Rosetta's pioneering music, in what was, technically speaking, the first rock and roll performance in history.

With her unprecedented and distinct style, Rosetta was the first to *do* rock and roll—even if the name of the genre had not yet been coined.

Her reputation at the time was widely revered among Black audiences, so much so that, in 1951, she held her third wedding at Washington, DC's, Griffith Stadium with twenty-five thousand paying audience members and a massive display of fireworks. Furthermore, when Chuck Berry was inducted into the Rock and Roll Hall of Fame in 1986, he said, "My career was one long Sister Rosetta Tharpe impersonation." Even Elvis was said to have been inspired by her pioneering guitar picking.

But as Rosetta's infectious energy and unique rhythms caught wind, both Black and white male musicians brought her sounds and vigorous styles into the mainstream music world. So as the fame of acts like Little Richard and Jerry Lee Lewis rose, Rosetta's fell. Although she was one of the first to popularize the electric guitar, and her pioneering music, energy, and performances provided the blueprint for generations of rock and roll icons to come, upon her death in 1973, she—and Arizona Dranes, too—was buried in an unmarked grave in Philadelphia and soon largely erased from music history. Only in 2018, nearly a century after she invented rock and roll, was she inducted into the Rock and Roll Hall of Fame.

# Willie Mae Thornton, aka Big Mama Thornton

***1926–1984***

JUST SAY THE WORDS "HOUND DOG," AND A mental image of Elvis Presley, with his white-bedazzled jumpsuit, coiffed black hair, and sultry stare, likely comes to mind. But Elvis is far from the original singer of his most recognizable and successful song. As the Rock and Roll Hall of Fame states, Elvis's version of "Hound Dog" is "the most illustrative example of the white appropriation of African-American music." The song was actually written for, and first performed by, Big Mama Thornton.

Willie Mae Thornton, better known as Big Mama Thornton, was a powerhouse blues musician and a pioneering legend of rock and roll who followed in the footsteps of the original rock and roll trailblazer, Sister Rosetta Tharpe. Born in the rural town of Ariton, Alabama, in 1926, Willie Mae, like Rosetta, grew up in the church. Her father was a Baptist minister, and her mother sang in the congregation. While Willie Mae would claim throughout her life that she did not often participate in the church services, she was a gifted musician who sang and played the harmonica and drums.

In 1940, at the age of fourteen, Willie Mae was discovered by Atlanta music promoter Sammy Green. Her mother had died that same year, so she left with Sammy and spent the next seven years touring the South as a blues singer with the Sammy Green Hot Harlem Review. Afterward, she settled in Houston, Texas, a city known at the time for its rich culture of Black music, including blues, jazz, zydeco, and country. It was there, in 1951, that she signed with her first label: Peacock Records.

By the age of twenty-six, Big Mama Thornton stood at over six feet tall and often dressed in men's clothing, and the 1950s American public had never seen anything like her. After meeting Willie Mae, the well-regarded lyricist Jerome Leiber said in an interview with *Rolling Stone* that she "looked like the biggest, baddest, saltiest chick you would ever seen [*sic*]." Jerome and his musical partner, the composer Mike Stoller, soon set out to create a song just for Willie Mae and her unique, big, badass personality.

The result? "Hound Dog." The song's iconic chorus quickly became a legendary euphemism calling out a man who was up to no good, and Big Mama Thornton's record, released in 1952, was

a hit too. It stayed on the R&B chart for fourteen weeks, sold over five hundred thousand copies, and had spurred more than ten covers by various musicians by the time Elvis came along.

But when Elvis recorded and released the song four years later, in 1956, it sold ten million copies and topped the three major charts (pop, country, and R&B) for eleven straight weeks, setting a new record that remained in place for the next three decades. "Hound Dog" skyrocketed Elvis to worldwide fame. It was the best-selling record of his entire career, and earned him—as well as Jerome and Mike, who received royalties—millions. In reviews or covers of Elvis's hit, neither Big Mama Thornton's version of the song nor her role as its inspiration were ever mentioned. And throughout her entire life, she reportedly earned no more than five hundred dollars in total for the record.

This practice of white artists cashing in on Black creativity was nothing new. It began decades earlier, with jazz in the 1930s and gospel and blues in the 1940s, and it continues to this day. However, when Big Mama Thornton released "Hound Dog," the music charts, like American society, were also still segregated. The "Rhythm and Blues Records" chart that her song topped had previously been known as "Race Records," the same chart where Sister Rosetta Tharpe's "Strange Things Happen Every Day" had been a hit. Although the name was changed, the stigmas remained; so, to cross a "Black" hit over to a "mainstream" audience, white performers would copy and cover the hits from the R&B charts. As Sam Phillips, the founder of Sun Records (Elvis's first record label), once said: "If I could find a white man who had the Negro sound and the Negro feel, I could make a billion dollars." And he did. Elvis and "Hound Dog" successfully crossed the colored line in America.

After "Hound Dog," Big Mama Thornton continued making music and touring. She also wrote some of her own songs, including "Ball and Chain," which self-proclaimed Big Mama Thornton fan Janis Joplin covered in her 1968 chart-topping album *Cheap Thrills*. Now lauded as one of Janis's greatest hits, Willie Mae was reportedly never asked permission for using the song, was never compensated for it, and her original version remains largely unknown.

What's more is that, unbeknownst to most, Big Mama Thornton was one of the first musicians—regardless of race or gender—to lay the groundwork for the wild, sexually liberated rock-star identity. Her tremendous presence, androgenous looks, and hard-partying lifestyle were unheard of at the time. But her lifestyle eventually caught up with her, and Willie Mae died in 1984 at just fifty-seven in extreme poverty. Buried in an unmarked grave, just like Sister Rosetta Tharpe, she died without receiving much credit for the bold path she had forged. Only decades later, in 2018, was Big Mama Thornton inducted into the Blues Hall of Fame, and she is yet to be recognized in any capacity by the Rock and Roll Hall of Fame.

# Taking to the Streets

## *Women played vital roles in civil rights activism*



The American Civil War resulted in the 13th Amendment, abolishing slavery in 1865. Soon after, the 14th Amendment gave citizenship to all people born in the US and the 15th Amendment gave Black men the right to vote. Yet it would take a century-long civil rights struggle to secure federal protection of these rights.

The American civil rights movement finally rose to national prominence in the 1950s, a time when the South was still segregated and Black people across the country remained subjects of violence and bigotry. Vigilant protests, sit-ins, and marches were happening across the country. The civil rights movement had spanned a century, yet two events that happened within one decade catalyzed major advancements: *Brown v. Board of Education*, a case heard in 1954 at the Supreme Court, and the 1963 March on Washington for Jobs and Freedom.

The impacts of these events on history are as famous as the men who spearheaded them. Thurgood Marshall won *Brown v. Board of Education*, making the segregation of schools—and in turn, all public services—unconstitutional. Martin Luther King Jr. led the March on Washington and changed the course of history with his "I Have a Dream" speech, but the march was also organized by five other men; together they are known as The Big Six.

The greatness and bravery of these men cannot be questioned. However, there are significant elements missing from the popularized histories of these two events—and both have to do with women being left out of the narratives.

Regarding *Brown v. Board of Education,* Thurgood did indeed carry the defense of Black American civil rights to monumental victory, but often overlooked is the basis of his defense: the legal treatise *States' Laws on Race and Color,* which was written by his legal peer Reverend Dr. Anna Pauli Murray, a trailblazing lawyer and civil rights activist in her own right.

And when it comes to the March on Washington, two women were actually embedded within the organizing committee: Anna Arnold Hedgeman and Dorothy Height. Anna recruited over 30,000 white attendees and only one woman stood behind Martin Luther King Jr. as he delivered his speech: Dorothy. Both Anna and Dorothy have been remembered as influential members of the civil rights and women's rights movements, but the Big Six should, in fact, be known as the Big Eight.

# Pauli Murray

***1910–1985***

FOR THE FIRST HALF OF THE 20TH CENTURY, public schools in the United States were legally allowed to be segregated, so long as the separate facilities were "equal." The "separate but equal" doctrine resulted from the trial of *Plessy v. Ferguson* in which the US Supreme Court ruled in 1896 that laws banning African Americans from sharing public spaces—buses, schools, restaurants, etc.—with white people were constitutionally sanctioned if there was an "equal" alternative. But the concept of "equal" is subjective, and these laws ushered in what is referred to as the inhumane Jim Crow era, especially in the South. And they stood for nearly six decades.

But the 1950s saw a turning point. The National Association for the Advancement of Colored People (NAACP) began a legal battle against segregation in public schools, filing lawsuits in states across the country. In 1951, when a young girl, Linda Brown, was told she could not attend the all-white elementary schools in Topeka, Kansas, her father, Oliver Brown, filed a class-action lawsuit against the Board of Education of Topeka. He claimed that schools for Black students were inferior to those for white children, and that segregation violated the 14th Amendment's so-called "equal protection clause."

The case was first heard at the US District Court in Kansas, which upheld segregation. But in 1952, it, along with four other cases related to the segregation of schools, went to the Supreme Court, which grouped them together under the name *Brown v. Board of Education Topeka.* The case was argued by Thurgood Marshall, head of the NAACP Legal Defense and Educational Fund. After a two-year battle, Thurgood won: Justice Earl Warren issued the verdict, writing that "in the field of public education the doctrine of 'separate but equal' has no place," and that segregated schools are "inherently unequal."

Though it took a number of years for schools to become truly integrated, the ruling was pivotal in encouraging the American Civil Rights movement.

However, the telling of this story is incomplete without including that of Dr. Pauli Murray, a trailblazing legal theorist, labor organizer, activist, poet, writer, and Episcopal priest, who wrote what became the foundations of Thurgood's defense in *Brown v. Board of Education.*

Pauli, from the time she was born as Anna Pauline Murray in 1910 until her death in 1985, used the discrimination she faced as both a Black person and a woman to fuel her life's work. She taught herself to read by age five and by fifteen had graduated from high school, where she wore many hats as the editor-in-chief of the school newspaper, the president of the literary society, the class secretary, a member of the debate club, the valedictorian, and a forward on the basketball team. She always chose to walk instead of taking a segregated bus, and boycotted movie theaters instead of succumbing to sitting in the balconies that were reserved for Black people. She became the first woman to attend law school at Howard University, where, on the first day of class in 1941, a professor announced he didn't know why a woman would want to attend law school. At that moment, she swore to herself "that I would become the top student," and termed this type of discrimination "Jane Crow." She worked just as hard to end this as she did Jim Crow.



With this mindset, Pauli was also often ahead of her time. In 1940, she was arrested for refusing to move to the back of a bus in Petersburg, Virginia—fifteen years before Rosa Parks. In 1943, she organized peaceful sit-ins in Washington, DC—twenty years before the famous Greensboro sit-ins. And in her final law-school paper, she argued that segregation violated the 13th and 14th Amendments of the US Constitution—a decade before the landmark case of *Brown v. Board of Education* was won.

That final paper grew from an idea her peers had initially laughed at. She and her classmates at Howard University were discussing how to bring an end to the Jim Crow era. They knew there was no such thing as "separate but equal," but lawyers had, until then, been focused on making things "equal." Instead of this approach, Pauli thought, why not rather focus on the "separate" aspect of the doctrine? Her classmates found this impractical and reckless—any challenge to *Plessy v. Ferguson*, they said, would result in the Supreme Court affirming it. But Pauli wasn't convinced. In fact, she was so sure of her argument that she bet her professor, Spottswood Robinson, ten dollars that the case would be overturned within twenty-five years.

After graduating from Howard, where she was not just the only woman in her class but also valedictorian, Pauli went to Berkeley for her Master of Laws degree before moving to New York City. At the time, only around a hundred African American women were practicing law in the entire country, and very few firms wanted to hire them; most of the jobs Pauli received were one-offs. One such gig came from the Women's Division of Christian Service of the Methodist Church in 1948: they opposed segregation and wanted to know where they were legally obliged to adhere to it and where it was merely customary, so they asked Pauli to write an explanation of segregation laws in America, and she accepted.

What Pauli produced was a 746-page document titled *States' Laws on Race and Color.* Made available by the Methodist Church in 1951, it expanded on ideas first outlined in her law-school paper, exposing the extent and absurdity of segregation in the United States through detailing the laws in place in 1950 across the country. It caught the attention of the American Civil Liberties Union, who distributed copies to law libraries, Black colleges, and human rights organizations, as well as the NAACP. Thurgood Marshall kept stacks of it in the office and, when building the case for *Brown v. Board of Education,* referred to it as "the bible."

But when Thurgood successfully won the case and *Plessy* was overturned in just ten years, Spottswood owed Pauli a lot more than ten dollars.

Some years after Pauli's graduation, Spottswood had joined Thurgood and other activists and lawyers to further discuss what he and Pauli's class had talked about: how to end segregation. During the conversation, he remembered Pauli's argument. He then found a copy of her paper and presented it to Thurgood and his team. Yet it wasn't until the late 1950s, years after the case had been won, that Pauli learned that her paper, and her tome, had formed the foundations of Thurgood's defense.

Pauli lived the rest of her life deeply embedded in the Civil Rights and Women's Rights movements. In 1966, she and more than twenty others came together to found the National Organization for Women. In 1971, when Ruth Bader Ginsburg won the case *Reed v. Reed,* which ruled that discrimination "on the basis of sex" was unconstitutional, her arguments rested on Pauli's work—so much so that Ruth named Pauli as a co-author on the brief. Then, in 1977, Pauli became the first female priest in the Episcopal Church.

Despite her prolific and groundbreaking contributions to fight against discrimination based on both skin color and sex, Pauli has only recently started to gain posthumous recognition. In 2016, her childhood home was designated a National Historic Landmark by the Department of the Interior, and in 2017, a residential college was named after her at Yale University, where, in 1965, she was the first African American to earn a Doctor of Jurisprudence. Beyond such acts of commemoration, her name should be taught and recognized hand in hand with those of Thurgood Marshall and *Brown v. Board of Education:* her ideas and writings are what provided the foundational argument that brought about an end to segregation in the United States.

WE DEMAND
AN END TO BIAS NOW!
WE DEMAN
EQUAL RIGHTS NOW!

# Anna Arnold Hedgeman and Dorothy Height

***1899–1990; 1912–2010***

ON AUGUST 28, 1963, MORE THAN 260,000 people gathered in the capital of the United States near the Lincoln Memorial. The occasion was the March on Washington for Jobs and Freedom, a peaceful demonstration advocating for the civil and economic rights of African Americans; it was where ten men gave speeches, including Martin Luther King Jr.'s now-iconic "I Have a Dream" speech, and where eleven men posed for countless photos in front of the memorial. Not a single woman's voice was heard, except for Mahalia Jackson's when she sang the national anthem. Six of the men who gave speeches are also remembered as the march's organizing committee, collectively referred to as the Big Six. But alongside these men worked two women, without whom the march would not have had the impact it did. Their names are Anna Arnold Hedgeman and Dorothy Height.

Anna was born in 1899 in Marshalltown, Iowa, and later moved to Anoka, Minnesota, where she and her family were the only African Americans in town. Her father stressed the importance of education, religion, and hard work, so when Anna finished high school in 1918, she became the first African American to attend—and later graduate from—Hamline University in Saint Paul, Minnesota. Despite having a BA in English, she was unable to find a job at a public school because she was Black; she eventually accepted a position at a historically Black college in Holly Springs, Mississippi.

Moving to the South was a rude awakening for Anna, and her first encounter with the Jim Crow segregation laws happened before she even arrived. Although she could sit anywhere during her journey by train from St. Paul to Chicago, she was told she'd have to move to the "colored" car as soon as she reached Cairo, Illinois. This car was filled with broken seats, overcrowded, and dirty, located directly behind the train's engine. Anna stayed in Mississippi for only two years before returning to the North, but, still unable to find a job teaching, she pivoted careers. In 1924, Anna started working for the Young Women's Christian Association (YWCA), which, at the time, had separate facilities for Blacks and whites. She eventually became an executive director and worked at different locations in Ohio, New Jersey, New York, and Pennsylvania.

Around this time, a teenaged Dorothy Irene Height, who was born in 1912 in Richmond,

Virginia, was volunteering in anti-lynching and voting-rights campaigns. Deeply engaged in civil rights work, she entered an oratory contest while in high school and delivered a speech on the Reconstruction—or post Civil War—Amendments (specifically, the 13th, 14th, and 15th), which had been established to abolish slavery, grant equal rights to formerly enslaved people, and enshrine the right to vote for people of all races. The jury awarded her first prize: a four-year college scholarship. Dorothy was planning to go to Barnard, but shortly before her first semester should've started, she was told she'd have to defer her attendance, as the school had already met their quota of two Black students for the year. Determined to start college, she took her acceptance letter to New York University, which didn't have a "diversity quota" and let her enroll. She earned a Bachelor's in Education from NYU in 1933, followed by a Master's in Psychology two years later. Dorothy—like Anna—started working at the YWCA, and by the late 1930s became the assistant executive director of the organization's Harlem location.

In the wake of Anna's work for the YWCA, Dorothy served as a consultant on racial issues for what is now known as the Department of Welfare, and, in 1946, she even became the executive director of Harry S. Truman's presidential re-election campaign, where she successfully re-enlisted Black Americans in the effort. Then, in 1954, she became the first African American woman to hold a mayoral cabinet position in New York City. At the same time, Dorothy herself had a brush with the presidency, when, at twenty-five, she was selected to escort then First Lady Eleanor Roosevelt to a meeting of the National Council of Negro Women, along with the council's founder, Mary McLeod Bethune. Mary subsequently became a mentor to Dorothy, and Dorothy also became a member of the YWCA's national leadership team, where she helped oversee the desegregation of its facilities in 1946. A year later, she also became president of Delta Sigma Theta, an international sorority for Black women.

By the 1950s, both Anna and Dorothy had established names and reputations for themselves as two of the most important women in the Civil Rights movement.

So, a few years later, when Dr. Martin Luther King Jr. and Asa Philip Randolph, leader of the Brotherhood of Sleeping Car Porters, were conceptualizing the March on Washington for Jobs and Freedom, they turned to Anna and Dorothy for their help, along with four other men: James Farmer, founder of the Congress of Racial Equality; John Lewis, president of the Student Nonviolent Coordinating Committee; Roy Wilkins, executive secretary of the National Association for the Advancement of Colored People; and Whitney Young, executive director of the National Urban League.

Throughout the entire process of planning the march, Anna and Dorothy were right there beside this group of men (known as the Big Six), offering strategic advice and organizational help. Due to Anna's political experience, leadership, and religious affiliations, she was responsible for recruiting over thirty thousand white attendees, and she also ensured that everyone in attendance had enough food and water. Moreover, during Martin Luther King Jr.'s speech, only one woman stood behind him: Dorothy. Anna and Dorothy also argued for more women to be involved in the process and spoke out when neither of them, nor any other woman, was given a turn to speak at the podium.

"Even on the morning of the march there had been appeals to include a woman speaker," Dorothy wrote in her 2003 autobiographical memoir, *Open Wide the Freedom Gates*. Although their efforts that day were futile, they were not entirely in vain, as Dorothy continued: "That moment was vital to awakening the women's movement. [It] showed us that men honestly didn't see their position as patriarchal or patronizing. They were happy to include women in the human family, but there was no question as to who headed the household!"

The day after the march, Dorothy organized a meeting where women in the Civil Rights movement could address both racism and sexism.

Anna and Dorothy had become acutely aware of this double-edged sword: they were marginalized in women's rights discussions because of their race, and pushed aside by Black groups because of their sex. The March on Washington marked an important turning point, after which they publicly advocated for African American and Women's Rights simultaneously, becoming two of the first women to confront discrimination from an intersectional approach.

In the mid-1950s, Dorothy had been named president of the National Council of Negro Women, a position she held until the early 1990s. In 1965, she was also appointed to head the newly established Office of Racial Justice at the YWCA, where she stayed until her retirement in 1977. And a year later, in 1966, Anna was one of over twenty women who together cofounded the National Organization for Women.

Both women were honored and are remembered for their fights for equality. Anna received the Pioneer Woman Award in 1983 and was given honorary doctorate degrees by Howard and Hamline universities. A portrait of her hangs in the National Portrait Gallery in Washington, DC. Dorothy also received multiple honorary degrees—from Harvard, Princeton, and Barnard, among others. In 1994, she was awarded a Presidential Medal of Freedom by President Bill Clinton, and in 2004 she received the Congressional Gold Medal from President George W. Bush. Then, in 2009, Dorothy was even given a place of honor onstage at the presidential inauguration of Barack Obama, who, when Dorothy died the next year, called her "the godmother of the Civil Rights movement and a hero to so many Americans." Yet despite these multiple awards and remembrances, the fact remains: the Big Six actually should be known as the Big Eight.

Down to Earth

*From land to sea, the planet is better understood thanks to these women*



We live on planet Earth, but much of the natural world around us has remained as much a mystery to humankind as the far-out reaches of the universe. For millions of years, earthquakes, tsunamis, and hurricanes were often interpreted as the lashing out of angered deities. The ocean was a feared force, just as willing to swallow seamen into its abyss as it was a source of life, providing endless sustenance for coastal communities. Gods lived at the tops of the highest mountains, far out of reach from the human civilizations below. Only in the past few centuries have the mysteries of land and sea begun to be unlocked. And only in the past few decades have areas of scientific study that focus on the earth—like geology, meteorology, oceanography, and seismology—advanced significantly with the help of modern technology.

A few thousand years ago, all life on Earth, be it animals, insects, or plants, were believed to be hand-created by the Christian god. This only started to change with the work of Charles Darwin, who is credited as being the biologist to first explore and document creatures around the world, which led to the acceptance of the theory of evolution—as well as his title of "the father of evolution." However, decades before Charles there was Maria Sibylla Merian, a naturalist who led one of the world's first scientific expeditions and laid the groundwork for her successor.

And then, when fossils of ancient creatures were first uncovered, people could not conceive that gigantic, now-extinct species really had lived on land and in the sea millions of years ago. Now, however, we know this to be fact, largely thanks to Mary Anning, who developed the field of paleontology before the term was even invented.

When it comes to the ocean, which covers 70 percent of Earth, our knowledge remains staggeringly thin. According to the National Oceanic and Atmospheric Administration (NOAA), 80 percent of the ocean remains unmapped, unexplored, and unobserved. But, due to the work of cartographer and oceanographer Marie Tharp, who helped create the first map of the ocean floor and revealed what today is considered its most defining feature, oceanic exploration was able to advance.

Finally, the Global Positioning System (GPS) revolutionized not only research across the scientific landscape but also the daily workings of society at large. Having an up-to-date, always-accessible map of any location on Earth was transformative—and an innovation which would not have been possible without the brainpower of Gladys Mae West.

# Maria Sibylla Merian

*1647–1717*

MARIA SIBYLLA MERIAN DID NOT PLAY with dolls as a child. Well, maybe she did, but more important to her was caring for silkworms, caterpillars, and other small insects. At the age of thirteen, she collected and even raised such creatures, observed them closely, and then painted them in great detail. She waited patiently for magical moments—when a caterpillar formed its cocoon or emerged as a butterfly—and rendered them in their vibrant, albeit natural, hues. More than their anatomy, she was interested in their entire life cycles: when and how insects came to life, how they grew and evolved.

Maria's lifelong obsession with the observation of the nonhuman living world was at a time when scientists still accepted Aristotle's theory of "spontaneous generation," first developed around 350 BCE. They believed maggots were created from rotten meat; insects grew from dew, mud, and even books; moths came from old wool; and caterpillars were produced by cabbages. The year was 1660.

From her teens into early adulthood, Maria continued to paint natural life. She recorded observations made in natural environments, creating intricate works of art showing caterpillars feeding on their host plants and predatory animals feeding on their prey. She showed a silkworm feeding on a mulberry bush; painted the silkworm moths as eggs, as hatching larvae, as molts and cocoons, and their final emergence as adult moths. She even distinguished between male and female. Meanwhile, scientists of the time confined themselves to labs, making drawings from preserved specimens. Maria was recording the ecology of countless species—nearly two centuries before the word "ecology" even existed—and by the end of the 1660s, her work had disproved the idea of spontaneous generation.

Maria was born in 1647 in Frankfurt am Main, Germany, and spent her early life moving around the country with her mother and stepfather, the artist Jacob Marrel, from whom she learned to paint. As an adult, following a failed marriage, she settled with her two daughters in Amsterdam, where, unlike many other countries at the time, women were permitted to pursue business endeavors and earn their own money. She sold her drawings to collectors, who in turn opened their cabinets of curiosities from around the world for her to see. Captivated by some of the creatures she saw, she decided that observing them pinned to boards wasn't enough: Maria needed to see them alive, in their natural habitats.

In 1699, at age fifty-two, Maria set sail with her youngest daughter to Surinam, then a Dutch colony on the northwest coast of South America. The two-month-long journey was one of the very first purely scientific expeditions in all of history, and she financed it by selling her art. Once there, the Dutch colonists did not believe two unaccompanied women could possibly be on a serious expedition and dismissed their intentions as frivolous. So instead of finding allies in the Europeans, Maria began working with enslaved

African and indigenous peoples (she herself never enslaved any people, and she also credited those who helped her in her published works). They brought her specimens, shared their knowledge about the medicinal and culinary benefits of certain plants, and cleared paths for her in the dense jungles and rain forests.

For two years, Maria made countless observations and drawings in Surinam. When she returned to Amsterdam, she published what is now regarded as her magnum opus, *Metamorphosis insectorum Surinamensium*. The book was written in Latin, the standard scientific language of the era, and featured sixty copperplate engravings. Azure butterflies hover over blossoms, ants crawl up branches, frogs watch over their eggs and tadpoles. Her drawings were not only stunning, but also true to life: blossoms had holes; blooms had lost their petals.



The publication of *Metamorphosis* garnered interest from scientists across Europe, who Maria then corresponded with. It, along with her other works, such as *Der raupen wunderbarer Verwandlung* (*The Wondrous Transformation of Caterpillars*), were displayed in prestigious libraries. The acclaimed Swedish naturalist Carl Linnaeus later used Maria's work to identify and classify insects—work that Maria herself had no interest in. Even Goethe, Germany's most celebrated poet, praised Maria for her ability to move "between art and science, between nature observation and artistic intention." Maria's focus on not just nonhuman species but their relationships with their surroundings went on to influence naturalists for decades to come.

At the turn of the 18th century, however, acclaim for Maria and her work was replaced with criticism and scorn. Scientists claimed she had misrepresented the natural world, and that her work was that of a fantastical imagination rather than scientific observation. Shoddy reproductions in her work, along with setbacks to women's rights in Europe, especially in Victorian-era England, resulted in her efforts being largely forgotten. In a book published in the 1830s, naturalist Lansdown Guilding described her work as "careless," "worthless," "vile," and "useless," and accused her of ignoring facts that "every boy entomologist would know." From this time onward, Maria "sort of dropped into oblivion," as biologist Dr. Kay Etheridge remarked in 2016. "Victorians started putting women in a box, and they're still trying to crawl out of it," she continued.

Indeed, much of Maria's work is still in need of rediscovery and restoration—not to mention that her place in natural-history books remains largely unwritten. But what we do know for certain is that she directly influenced Linnaeus's systems of taxonomy. And as journalist Andrea Wolf observed, "150 years before Charles Darwin wrote his *Origin of Species*, [Maria Sibylla] Merian knew nature well enough to depict it as a constant struggle for survival."

# Mary Anning

***1799–1847***

THE TONGUE TWISTER "SALLY SELLS SEA-shells by the seashore" might be well-known, but what isn't so well-known is the fact that the character Sally was inspired by a real-life Mary—Mary Anning, one of the earliest pioneers of geology and one of the first people to make important paleontological discoveries.

Born in the coastal resort town of Lyme Regis, England, Mary grew up walking along the shore with her brother, mother, and father. Together, they would look for shells, collect and clean them, and then, like the tongue twister says, sell them to tourists. Yet these were no ordinary shells; they were what are now called ammonites, or fossilized remains of prehistoric mollusks. Due to their unusual appearance, locals, including the Anning family, called them "curiosities," and tourists were fascinated.

When Mary's father died suddenly and unexpectedly, her older brother Joseph became a carpenter's apprentice, and the business of selling such curios was left to her. The siblings earned a meager income, barely enough to feed themselves and their mother, but Mary recognized that the "shells" she found were important, and she went out of her way to collect more.

As she grew older, she wandered from beaches to the fossils' direct source: the surrounding limestone-and-shale cliffs. Landslides often occurred during the region's harsh winter months, revealing new land and, with it, new fossils. To collect them, Mary used a technique she'd learned from her father, who would see a peculiarly round lump of rock, climb up a steep cliff, set down his basket, hammer a chisel into the crumbling wall, and pry the spiral-shaped stones away. Working in such a dangerous environment, Mary took great risks and had to maneuver quickly; although she was never seriously injured, in 1833 her dog Trey died during a particularly bad landslide.

Mary's fastidiousness and fearlessness led her in 1811, when she was only twelve years old, to her first groundbreaking discovery. After a big storm, Joseph found the remains of an unusual-looking skull, which prompted Mary to excavate the surrounding area. In her quest, she found and recovered a full seventeen-foot-long fossilized skeleton of what appeared to be a sea dragon.

Word about her discovery spread quickly, and she soon received visits from scientists and

university professors. At first, the scientists believed it to be some kind of crocodile. After all, Georges Cuvier, known as the "father of paleontology," had only recently introduced the theory of extinction, and Charles Darwin's groundbreaking book *On the Origin of Species* would not be published for another forty-eight years. For most, the ideas that life had existed millions of years before Biblical times and that a species could go extinct were inconceivable.

The discovery of this otherworldly "crocodile" was only the beginning for Mary. She would find many more such creatures; and in 1823, when she was twenty-four years old, she discovered an even more unusual skeleton—one that was nine feet long and six feet wide with a head that was less than five inches long. So strange was this new specimen that rumors developed about its being a fake, Georges himself among those supporting the accusation. The Geological Society of London held a lengthy meeting to discuss its validity, although Mary was not invited. Eventually, Georges admitted his misjudgment and the fossil was recognized as the skeleton of a new species: the Plesiosaurus, meaning "near to reptile."

Five years later, in 1828, Mary made another stunning discovery: the skeleton of what looked like a flying dragon. Along with the "crocodiles" she had found, these bones were studied at length and were determined to be the oldest prehistoric creatures. Far from being crocodiles, her earlier discoveries were named ichthyosaur, meaning "fish lizard," and the latter pterodactyl, meaning "wing finger."

Mary's first ichthyosaur and the pterodactyl were purchased by a museum, and geologists bought her other findings. Yet the upper-class London gentlemen who dominated the emerging field of geology did not take Mary, a provincial lower-class woman, seriously; her name was omitted from the scientific articles discussing her findings, as well as the museum displays showcasing them. Credit for her findings was consistently given to the men who had purchased them.

Moreover, the payments for her fossils were minimal, and she and her family continued to struggle financially. At one point, the family was so desperate that Mary's mother wrote letters begging a curator at the British Museum to pay for an ichthyosaur he had taken but for which he had never sent the money.

However, the importance of Mary's work eventually became too great to ignore. News of her discoveries traveled around the world and led her to correspond with some of the best and most well-known academics of her time. Occasionally collectors and scholars from as far away as North America would travel to Lyme Regis to tour her excavations or to get her expert opinion on their own geological work. After all, it was her commitment to fossil-hunting and her excavations that paved the way for the field of geology and the development of paleontology at a time before the word "dinosaur" existed. Because of Mary's findings, the scientific community learned that the earth was not merely thousands but rather hundreds of millions of years old—a realization that would influence Charles Darwin's theory of evolution decades later.

Toward the very end of her career, Mary was finally credited with her discoveries in scientific papers. Upon her death in 1847, after a two-year battle with breast cancer, she even received the only obituary ever given by the Geological Society of London to someone who was not a member. Yet she—along with all women until 1904—was never allowed to join the Geological Society itself, and the acceptance and recognition given to her did not last long. After her death, her name was erased in history books and museums, and credit for her countless discoveries was re-ascribed to the various male fossilists who had purchased her finds.

Today, the shoreline of Lyme Regis is a UNESCO World Heritage Site known as the Jurassic Coast, and discoveries that follow in Mary's footsteps are still being made by amateurs and paleontologists alike. Yet Mary remains best recognized as Sally—a girl at the seashore, selling seashells.

# Marie Tharp

***1920–2006***

TODAY IT IS WIDELY ACCEPTED THAT THE earth's outermost surface comprises a number of large tectonic plates, or individual pieces of land that have been slowly shifting for the last 3.4 billion years. As a result, we experience continental drift, the ever-so-slight but always-happening movement of Earth's seven continents and its ocean floors.

In the 1950s, however, this idea was vehemently rejected by the scientific community; believing in plate tectonics or continental drift was practically a form of scientific heresy. At the time, the commonly held belief was that the ocean floors were flat, featureless expanses, rather than mountainous, varied landscapes as diverse as those seen above water. So when, in 1953, cartographer Marie Tharp first identified a rift in the ocean floor she was mapping and presented it to her colleagues, her collaborator Bruce Heezen said, "It cannot be. It looks too much like continental drift." He then quickly dismissed the discovery as "girl talk."

Yet what Marie found, and what Bruce did not yet recognize, would forever alter the course of geology and ocean exploration. She had discovered the ten-thousand-mile-long Mid-Atlantic Ridge, a find that proved the seafloor was spreading.

Marie and Bruce worked closely together at the Lamont Geological Observatory, now the Lamont-Doherty Earth Observatory, at Columbia University. They were part of a team working with new sonar technologies used to measure the depths of the ocean. However, at the same time, women were not allowed on Navy boats, nor would their supervisor, Maurice Ewing, founder of the Lamont lab, permit women on research vessels. He believed a woman's presence at sea to be bad luck (so much so that when biologist Mary Sears, who had sneaked aboard a ship as a stowaway, was found, the ship was rerouted to land to drop her off). As such, Marie was resigned to working on land: for two decades, Bruce would go out on the ships, collect sonar data, and send it back to Marie in the lab. She then synthesized the data and produced visualizations of it, resulting in some of the world's first maps of ocean floors.

Marie's process was done in a pre-computer era. She worked with pens, ink, and rulers, painstakingly drawing underwater details, longitude degree by latitude degree, by hand on white linen, according to thousands of sonar readings. She aligned data not only from Bruce but from other ships too. At one point, she had amassed so much data that her map was printed on a scroll five

thousand feet long. It was thankless work, but she reveled in it. "I had a blank canvas to fill with extraordinary possibilities," Marie wrote in an essay in 1999. "It was a once-in-a-lifetime—a once-in-the-history-of-the-world—opportunity for anyone, but especially for a woman in the 1940s."

Marie, born in 1920 in Ypsilanti, Michigan, spent her childhood moving around frequently while her father, a soil surveyor, worked in the northern states in the summer and southern states in the winter. By the time she finished high school, she'd attended nearly two dozen schools. Encouraged to pursue a career like teaching, she attended Ohio University and graduated with majors in English and music.

But after Pearl Harbor was attacked, a door opened for women: for the first time, women were needed to fill the job vacancies left when men went to fight in World War II. One tangible result of this wartime workforce shortage was that the University of Michigan opened its geology department to female students, and Marie was one of ten young women who applied in 1943. She was accepted, earned a master's degree, and was then offered a job at Stanolind Oil and Gas Co. in Tulsa, Oklahoma. Searching for additional challenges, though, she soon enrolled at the University of Tulsa, earned another master's in math, and eventually embarked on a journey to New York City in search of a new job. In New York, she was hired by Maurice Ewing at Lamont as a draftsperson. At first, she worked for whoever needed her mapping skills, but as time went on, she began working almost exclusively with Bruce.

By the time Marie was identifying the first indications of the ridges and huge valley in the Atlantic Ocean in 1953, she knew to re-check her calculations time and again before sharing them with colleagues—she was, after all, no stranger to being disbelieved or belittled in a male-dominated field. But despite this, Bruce made her redo the calculations again, and when she came up with the same results, her discovery was still pushed aside.

With additional sonar data, Bruce himself went on to discover that earthquakes were taking place beneath the rift valley Marie had found. It wasn't until this development that he began to support Marie's hypothesis, and he soon announced their discoveries to the scientific community.

In 1956, Bruce and their supervisor, Maurice, presented the findings that showed sea spreading—which evinced continental drift—at a meeting of the American Geophysical Union in Toronto. (Unfortunately, it remains unclear whether Marie's contributions were mentioned during this presentation or if she was originally invited to be part of it herself; Marie was known to avoid the limelight, repeatedly declining opportunities to present her own work.) The following year, after Bruce gave a talk on the findings at Princeton University, the geologist Harry Hess stood up and said, "Young man, you have shaken the foundations of geology!" But overall, the scientific community's reactions varied from skepticism to amazement to scorn.

Marie and Bruce continued their work gathering data and mapping the ocean, and it eventually became clear that the rift Marie had found extended up and down the entire Atlantic Ocean—the Mid-Atlantic Ridge is, today, considered Earth's largest physical feature. By 1957, Marie and Bruce had pieced together the first full map of the Atlantic Ocean floor. Their work then went on to reveal a forty thousand–mile underwater ridge and series of mountain ranges that circled the entire globe. By the 1970s, Marie had produced the first map of the entire ocean floor.



But when Bruce announced their initial discovery in the '50s, it ignited heated arguments about the rift, and therefore continental drift. As the debate raged among her male colleagues, Marie resigned herself to cartography. "I was so busy making maps I let them argue. I figured I'd show them a picture of where the rift valley was and where it pulled apart," she said.

Having the same thought, another scientist, Jacques Cousteau, set out on a ship hoping to disprove Marie and Bruce by showing where the rift valley *wasn't*. He crossed the Atlantic Ocean on a research vessel—something Marie was still not allowed to do—with a movie camera on a sled near the seafloor in tow. To his dismay, the purported rift existed exactly where Marie said it did. Jacques, now also forced to believe Marie's findings, presented his stunning films of big black undersea cliffs at the first International Ocean Congress in New York in 1959. As is often said, a picture is worth a thousand words, and from then on, the scientific community-at-large began to accept Marie's rift valley as fact.

Yet as research on the rift valley, continental drift, and the theory of plate tectonics developed in the coming decades, Marie's name slowly but surely disappeared from the conversation. Not only that, but when Maurice and Bruce had an argument in 1968, Marie was fired in its wake; Bruce had a tenured position and therefore it was impossible to fire him, whereas she had a precarious position and became the scapegoat for her male colleagues' disagreement. Bruce ensured that Marie maintained an income via research grants, but she no longer had a space at the lab with other colleagues; she had to move her map-making endeavors to her home.

Before she died in 2006, Marie was remembered and honored as a brilliant cartographer who indeed produced groundbreaking maps of the earth's entire ocean floor. But her initial vindication of the then-controversial theory of continental drift was ultimately forgotten. Instead, in Marie's place, people like Maurice and Harry, along with other men like William Morgan, Walter Pitman, Lynn Sykes, and Dan McKenzie, who built directly on her hypothesis and maps, are remembered as founding fathers of the now-accepted theory of plate tectonics.

# Gladys Mae West

***1930–***

THE GLOBAL POSITIONING SYSTEM, OR GPS, is a fundamental part of modern life. A satellite-based navigation system, it is used in every aspect of our globalized society, from smartphones and cars to space programs and military operations to aviation and even social media platforms. In short, the invention of GPS was nothing short of revolutionary. But while the National Inventors Hall of Fame credits physicists Ivan Getting and Roger Eaton, along with engineer Col. Bradford Parkinson, as its inventors, the fact is that the foundations for GPS were laid decades before these men received this recognition in the early aughts—and they were laid by a woman: Gladys Mae West.

Born in 1930, Gladys is from an agricultural family in a community of sharecroppers. Her parents owned a small farm in Sutherland, Virginia, where she helped pick corn, cotton, and tobacco from a young age, though she also had a love and talent for mathematics. Encouraged by her teachers, she saw math as a potential path out of agriculture. "I was gonna get an education and I was going to get out of there," she said in an interview in 2020. "I wasn't going to be stuck there all my life." So, Gladys poured her spare time and energy into studying, and in 1948 she graduated as valedictorian of her high school class, which earned her a full scholarship to Virginia State College (now Virginia State University).

Despite her talents, however, Gladys had a difficult time finding a job after receiving her bachelor's degree. Not only is math, to this day, a largely male-dominated field, but Gladys was also a Black woman in 1952 in a segregated state. After applying in vain for a number of government positions, she resigned herself to teaching math while simultaneously pursuing graduate studies. Three years later, she earned a master's degree from her alma mater, and again applied for jobs with the government. In 1956, she finally received an offer from the US Naval Weapons Laboratory, where she worked until she retired in 1998.

Once at the lab, Gladys was a minority—she was the second Black woman ever hired, and only the fourth Black employee—but that didn't deter her from carving a path of her own. She began her career as part of a small cohort of women mathematicians who did calculations by hand and verified tables for the military.

When a computer was later installed, she was given some programming training and

then began working with the Naval Ordnance Research Calculator. In this position, she helped program the research calculator to establish the motion of Pluto in relation to Neptune—a task that required five billion arithmetic calculations and a hundred hours of computer calculations—and from then on, Gladys's primary focus was on calculations for satellite orbits.

In 1978, the Navy launched the first Earth-orbiting satellite designed to remotely sense the earth's oceans, and Gladys was appointed project manager. She and her team used the satellite to measure ocean depths, data which could then be used to create highly accurate computer simulations of the earth's entire surface. Almost a decade later, in 1986, Gladys published a guide outlining how this data could additionally be used to calculate a geoid, or in other words, a mathematical model of the earth's shape.

Her geodetic Earth model was incredibly accurate, unlike anything previously produced. To generate it, she employed complex algorithms that took into account variations in gravitational, tidal, and other forces that determine and distort the shape of the earth. Her model—and, more importantly, its data—proved to be an essential building block of what would later become the GPS satellite orbit.

But at the time, Gladys had no inkling of the importance of her work and her name went unrecognized—that is until 2017, when she submitted a short biography to her college sorority Alpha Kappa Alpha for an alumni event.

Her bio sparked an interest among her sorority sisters, who were so enraptured by Gladys's work that they contacted the Associated Press. The AP took an interest in the story and published an article about Gladys's work in 2018. From there, the story spread quickly but relatively quietly: the US military deemed her a "hidden figure" of GPS history in a press release, and she was inducted into the US Air Force Hall of Fame, where she was recognized for her refined calculations and accurate geodetic Earth model that was "optimized for what ultimately became the Global Positioning System orbit."

However, Gladys is largely still a hidden figure in the mainstream history of GPS. And while Roger Easton was added to the National Inventors Hall of Fame for his contributions to GPS eight years after Ivan Getting and Col. Bradford Parkinson's initial induction, Gladys's name remains missing from its ranks.

# That’s One Small Step for Man, One Giant Leap for Womankind

*Women propelled the first man into space—*
*and humankind's understanding of the universe*



While early civilizations looked to the heavens and saw the unknown, they did recognize the movements of stars and planets. The patterns they observed influenced countless aspects of ancient life—from navigation to religion to architecture—but the exact mechanics of the phenomena they tracked remained mysteries for thousands of years.

Inquisitive minds continued to contemplate these puzzles and by the late 19th century much of the visible sky had been mapped and many far away phenomena had been deciphered. Then, in the 20th century, the technology behind telescopes and cameras further advanced, opening the night sky to science. Physicists began unraveling the secrets of the universe's unseen forces, like gravity and time, and humans would soon travel to space and even walk on the moon. And women were at the center of this cosmic story.

In the late 1800s, women were generally unwelcome in the workforce and academia. But the doors were cracked open at the Harvard Observatory when women were hired as human computers, tasked with identifying and classifying every known star. Today, these women are remembered as the Harvard Computers. Four of them—Willamina Fleming, Annie Cannon, Henrietta Leavitt, and Cecilia Gapochkin—transcended their clerical work, making discoveries and achieving astronomical feats that altered the fabric of astronomy and astrophysics.

Across the Atlantic, the name Einstein would soon become synonymous with the highest heights of human genius. But Albert's biography often omits Mileva Marić: Mileva was not just his first wife, but his collaborator and a genius in her own right. Without her, the Einstein legacy and the revolutionary equation $E = mc^2$ would not exist.

Nearly 100 years later, two women blasted open the boundaries of known astronomy, again altering the field forever. In 1964, Jocelyn Bell Burnel discovered radio pulsars—the tool needed to advance the study of gravity and black holes—and in 1974, Vera Rubin proved the existence of dark matter, which until then had only been considered a radical theory.

Around the same time, the Soviet Union and the United States were neck-in-neck in the Space Race. Both nations successfully launched men into outer space and, eventually, to the moon. While the male astronauts who made the journeys are household names, it wasn't until the 2010s that light was shed on Katherine Johnson, the woman who single-handedly calculated the trajectories that sent these men into orbit and to the moon.

# The Harvard Computers

***late 19th century–early 20th century***

THE WORD "COMPUTER" DID NOT ALWAYS refer to a digital, programmable electronic machine. Before the electronic era, there were human "computers," and the task of doing mathematical computations was considered secretarial work. As the majority of professional and academic realms were exclusively the domains of men, being a "computer" was one of the only jobs outside domestic work available to women.

In the late 19th century, a group of female computers at the Harvard College Observatory revolutionized the field of astronomy, with the most notable contributions made by Williamina Fleming, Annie Cannon, Henrietta Leavitt, and Cecilia Gaposchkin. But these women were only four of a group of about eighty who were ridiculed, unacknowledged, and often identified as merely "Pickering's girls" or "Pickering's harem," names made in reference to their supervisor, physicist and astronomer Edward Pickering.

Edward was the director of the Harvard Observatory from 1877 to 1918, and was progressive for the time. Previously, as a professor at the Massachusetts Institute of Technology, he had famously upended the scientific status quo by allowing students to participate in experiments, and he welcomed young women in his lectures. Hiring women extended his progressive path, but there were limits: Edward's computers earned half the rate a man would have earned, for women were not yet allowed to be formally recognized as scientists at Harvard (women weren't even allowed to enroll as students until 1950).

Edward was progressive as an astrophysicist, too: he was one of the first in the field to use photographs to conduct research. By connecting a camera to a telescope, and using a spectrograph to see the spectra of stars—in other words, a star's temperature, chemical composition, and luminosity—clear and accurate images of the night sky could be analyzed in perpetuity; astronomers no longer needed to always work at night or use only notes taken while making observations through the telescope. Edward also had an ambitious goal: he wanted to use astrophotography to define every star and map the entire night sky, and for the first time, it seemed possible. He invented a way to capture any star within the telescope's view on 8″× 10″ photographic plates. His vision would become the Henry Draper Catalogue, named after the amateur astronomer who made the first photograph of a star's spectrum and whose widow, Anna, funded Edward's project.

While working toward this goal, Edward needed help analyzing and cataloging the thousands of glass-plate photographs. But he was producing more data than his male assistants could handle and, moreover, he was not impressed with their work. So, in 1881, Edward handed off some of their work to his maid, Williamina Fleming. To his surprise, she was excellent and efficient at computing, and five years later, he began putting together an all-woman team of computers to process astronomical data and to classify stars.

Mainly male astronomers worked the telescopes and took the pictures, while the women tediously inspected, analyzed, and cataloged the images. First, some women would adjust the images to render the photographs as clearly and accurately as possible. Others would then use the photographs to classify the stars, measuring brightness, position, and color. Others then cataloged the pictures, carefully detailing the date of exposure and region of the sky. Finally, the notes were painstakingly copied in a table based on the star's magnitude and location.



However, four of Edward's computers—Williamina, Annie, Henrietta, and Cecilia—transcended clerical work and contributed to the very foundations of modern astronomy, becoming scientists in everything but title.

Williamina Fleming was born in 1857, in Scotland. She moved to Boston with her husband in 1878, when she was twenty-one years old and pregnant, but he abandoned her soon after their arrival. As a single mother, she needed to earn an income. So she became a maid and was hired to work in Edward's home in 1879.

Two years later, when Edward gave her data to analyze, Williamina became the first computer. She identified specific, recurring characteristics in all the stars' spectra and, using this information, she and Edward developed a classification system that categorized stars alphabetically, according to the strength of each star's hydrogen spectra lines, or how much hydrogen a star had. In 1890, the first edition of the *Draper Catalogue of Stellar Spectra* was published using this classification system: Williamina was responsible for classifying 28,266 spectra from 10,351 stars.

As office manager, Williamina also wrote, edited, and proofread data tables, reports, and research papers, and was responsible for hiring new staff. More importantly, throughout her career she discovered ten novae, fifty-nine gaseous nebulae, more than three hundred variable stars, the famous Horsehead Nebula, and the existence of white dwarfs (super-hot tiny stars). She also established the first photographic standards of magnitude, which is used to measure the fluctuating brightness of variable stars and remains a vital tool for astronomers today.

But Williamina's name was not included as a coauthor of the *Draper Catalogue*, and when the first edition of *The New General Catalogue of Nebulae and Clusters of Stars* had been published two years earlier, her name had also been removed from all her discoveries. With only Edward mentioned, Williamina's contributions to astronomy were erased.

Six years after the publication of the *Draper Catalogue*, in 1896, Annie Jump Cannon joined the Harvard Computers, becoming one of the first women in the group to have advanced degrees and prior experience in the field. Annie was born in Delaware in 1863 and had enrolled at Wellesley College, a top women's college, at age seventeen. She graduated as valedictorian with a physics degree in 1884, and later worked as an assistant to her former professor. During this time, she also completed a graduate degree and was introduced to spectroscopy and astrophotography.

So, when Annie became a computer, it was as Edward's assistant in the observatory. She spent her nights observing the sky, recording fluctuations in stars' brightness, but she was also a classification genius. In her career of over forty years, Annie identified and cataloged nearly 350,000 stars along with their spectra, and discovered more than three hundred variable stars, five novae, and one spectroscopic binary star. Furthermore, and most importantly, she devised her own star-classification system.

Williamina's classification system divided stars into fifteen spectral categories by hydrogen content. Edward's niece, who also worked as a computer, had come up with a more complicated classification system, with twenty-two categories that relied on a star's helium content. Annie created a compromise between the two systems: she ranked stars by temperature, from hottest to coldest, and, using the mnemonic "Oh, Be A Fine Girl, Kiss Me," divided stars into spectral classes O, B, A, F, G, K, and M.

Annie's system was officially adopted by the International Astronomical Union in 1922. However, unlike most scientific discoveries and inventions that are memorialized by being named after the scientist who did the work, Annie's system was called the Harvard Classification System—crediting the invention, to this day, to Harvard at large instead of to the scientist behind the development.

Then there was Henrietta Swan Leavitt, who was born in Massachusetts in 1868 and, when she was twenty, enrolled at the Society for the Collegiate Instruction of Women (later called Radcliffe College)—the women's program at Harvard, where attendees could not earn degrees but could listen to Harvard professors repeat lectures on a volunteer basis. She was hired as a computer in 1893, an opportunity that would lead her to become "the woman who discovered how to measure the universe."

At the observatory, Henrietta was tasked with studying variable stars. But, while identifying and cataloging data on these stars with changing brightnesses, Henrietta began to notice a pattern: the period of a star's brightness cycle, which relates to the size of the star, could be observed in relation to its absolute magnitude, or luminosity, which refers to the amount of energy the star emits per second. And, significantly, she could observe this phenomenon with accuracy and consistency.

Henrietta first published her discovery in the *Annals of the Astronomical Observatory of Harvard College* in 1908. Four years later, in 1912, she formally articulated this period-luminosity relationship as an astronomical truth. Now recording the brightness of a variable star and the period of its light pulsation made it possible, for the first time, to calculate a star's distance from Earth.

The impact of Henrietta's new measurement tool cannot be understated. Without it, Edward Hubble could not have realized, in 1924, that the Andromeda galaxy is not part of the Milky Way, proving that the universe has innumerable galaxies, not just one. Six years later, Harlow Shapley, Hubble's protégé and successor as director of the observatory, also built on Leavitt's Law when he realized that neither the earth nor the sun is in the center of the Milky Way galaxy, as was previously thought.

However, Hubble published Henrietta's finding under his own name in the *Harvard Circular* in 1912, stating that she had only prepared the finding, effectively taking credit for the achievement himself. Although her discovery is now sometimes referred to as Leavitt's Law, Henrietta never received credit during her lifetime and has never been officially recognized for it.

About a decade later, Cecilia Payne Gaposchkin became the next computer to make an impact far beyond secretarial duties. Cecilia joined the Harvard Observatory—now under the directorship of Harlow—at the age of twenty-three. She was born in 1900 in England and, having always had a penchant for learning, was offered a scholarship to Cambridge University in 1919. Cecilia studied astronomy and completed the program, but she never received a degree because Cambridge did not offer them to women until 1948. With few job prospects beyond teaching in England, Cecilia went to the US, where Harlow became keenly aware of Cecilia's intellectual prowess.

Soon after her arrival, Harlow encouraged Cecilia to write a doctoral dissertation, which resulted in her being awarded the first PhD to ever be given to a student of Radcliffe College. Her thesis, finished in 1925, outlined one of the greatest leaps in astronomical history: by studying the spectral classes of stars and their temperatures, Cecilia determined the chemical composition of stars and, more significantly, that hydrogen is the most abundant element in the universe.

When Cecilia's dissertation was reviewed, however, astronomer Henry Norris Russell persuaded her not to present the conclusion as fact, because it was so vastly different from the accepted knowledge of the time. Cecilia listened to him and changed the verbiage of her dissertation to say that the finding was "spurious." But then, in 1929, four years later, Henry came to the same conclusion as Cecilia, albeit through different means, and published the finding as his own. Ever since, Henry has largely been given credit for the discovery.

Today, Williamina, Annie, Henrietta, and Cecilia—along with the other seventy-five or so women who worked alongside them—are collectively known as the Harvard Computers, and they have finally gained recognition as a pivotal force that allowed the Harvard Observatory to break the astronomical ground that it did. But some of these women deserve to be identified by name and recognized for the individual contributions they made, just like their male counterparts—for they were more than part of a collective hive mind; Williamina, Annie, Henrietta, and Cecilia had computational brains of their own.

Mileva Marić
1875–1948
E=mc²
E=mc²

THE NAME EINSTEIN IS, TODAY, A METONymy for genius; popular culture and history at large have crowned Albert Einstein as the exemplary case for human genius, and for how high our capacity for intelligence can ascend. Albert undoubtedly had a mind that transcended even most above-average people, and his mathematical and astrophysical theories not only expanded the possibilities of how scientists might be able to conceive universal forces, but almost all of them have also been proven to be true.

However, the myth of Einstein as a sole genius is not factual, for Albert did not toil away on his own. He worked and theorized alongside a collaborator: his first wife, Mileva Marić.

Mileva and Albert met in 1896 at the Polytechnic Institute in Zurich, Switzerland. They were two of five students in the physics and mathematics department, and Mileva was not just the only woman in the cohort; she was the first woman ever admitted to the school.

Mileva was born in 1875 in Titel, Vojvodina—which was then part of the Austro-Hungarian empire and is now an autonomous province of Siberia—and had always possessed a penchant for learning. She started high school in Titel, and her father, a wealthy and respected member of the community, was able to obtain authorization for her to attend physics lectures, which were usually restricted to boys. She loved math and science, and also learned Greek, French, and German. However, girls were soon banned from receiving an education beyond elementary school in her hometown, so Mileva's family sent her to boarding school in Switzerland, where women were also allowed to attend university.

When Mileva applied to the Polytechnic Institute, she breezed through the entrance exam on her first try. Albert, meanwhile, had to take it twice before he was admitted (and had even already failed entrance exams at three other schools). Shortly after they both arrived, they became inseparable. Letters and firsthand accounts recall the pair spending countless hours studying together. Mileva was organized and an avid learner who keenly attended lectures, while Albert disliked classes and preferred to study at home with Mileva. Her housemates remember Albert always being in her room, coming and going and borrowing books even in her absence.

At the end of their classes in 1900, Mileva and Albert had similar grades, varying by only tenths of a point, in everything but applied physics: she received a five (the top mark) and he only a one. But when it came time for the final oral exam in 1901, Albert and the three other male students received eleven points out of twelve, while she only got five—a failing grade. Some accounts state she was discriminated against by the evaluating male professor, which is very likely true. However, it's also true that in 1901 Mileva got pregnant out of wedlock, a scandal for the time; she left Zurich and gave birth to a daughter in Novi Sad, where her family was living (the fate of the child is unknown). Be it discrimination, personal reasons, or a combination thereof, Mileva never received a diploma.

Meanwhile, in 1900, Albert published a paper under only his name. Yet—as with many papers to come—letters sent by Albert and Mileva indicate that the paper was in fact a collaborative effort. Mileva, writing to a friend, said: "We sent a private copy to [Austrian physicist and philosopher Ludwig] Boltzmann [. . .] I hope he will answer us." Moreover, Albert wrote to Mileva that one of his friends visited "Prof. Jung, one of the most influential physicists in Italy, and gave him a copy of our article."



Similar to the story of Mileva's lack of a diploma, publishing a collaborative effort under only Albert's name could have had many reasons. First and foremost, in the early 1900s, women were not accepted as serious, intellectual scientists, so publishing a paper with a woman's name would have carried less weight. At the same time, Mileva desperately wanted to marry Albert, but to be eligible for marriage, he needed a job—and publishing a paper could have increased his chances. No matter the reasoning, this initial paper set the tone for the rest of their relationship: Mileva and Albert continued to collaborate, but her presence always disappeared in his shadow.

In the summer of 1902, Albert found work at a patent office in Bern, Switzerland. Six months later, in January 1903, the pair married. The following year, their first son, Hans-Albert, was born.

Then, in 1905, Albert had what history refers to as his "miracle year." He published five articles, commented on twenty-one scientific papers, and submitted his thesis. One of these articles eventually led to his 1921 Nobel Prize, and another was what made him a household name around the world: it included a theory of special relativity and the famous equation $E = mc2$.

In essence, the theory of special relativity explains how speed affects mass, time, and space. It also includes a way for the speed of light ($c$) to define the relationship between energy and matter: a small amount of mass ($m$), the article said, can be interchangeable with massive amounts of energy ($E$), as defined by the equation $E = mc2$. Importantly, the theory could only be applied to cases without gravity. Although he later added gravity to the concept, in 1915, with the publication of a paper on general relativity, the theory of special relativity was groundbreaking. It upended humans' understanding of how the universe works, especially with regard to time and how everything from a tangible object to light travels through space.

But there's proof that this theory was not Albert's alone.

In 1901, Albert wrote to Mileva: "How happy and proud I will be when the two of us together will have brought our work on relative motion to a victorious conclusion." What's more, three early drafts of the paper were allegedly signed "Einstein-Marity," the latter name being the Hungarian version of "Marić." Scholars still argue over the extent to which Mileva contributed to the theory, some even claiming that these facts are speculations. Yet other firsthand sources recall Albert frequently saying "I need my wife. She solves for me all my mathematical problems," and additional letters indicate their ongoing collaborations, always referring to "our" work.

After the miracle year, Albert started gaining recognition around Europe. He was asked to give lectures around the continent and held various faculty positions in Prague, Zurich, and Berlin. Although he rarely mentioned Mileva publicly, multiple pages of his lecture notes from this time are in her handwriting, as is a letter drafted in 1910 to the renowned German physicist and originator of quantum theory Max Planck, who had sought Albert's opinion.

But none of this was known until 1987, nearly forty years after Mileva's death, when her correspondences with Albert were published after being discovered in Hans-Albert's possession. Up until that point, Mileva's name had all but disappeared from history. For as Albert's fame rose, their marriage deteriorated, and he took the credit the world bestowed solely upon him and ran with it.

In 1910, Mileva gave birth to their second son, Eduard, but by 1912, Albert had started an affair with his cousin, and in 1914 the married couple formally separated. In February 1919, they were finally divorced, and that summer Albert married his cousin. In 1921, Albert won the Nobel Prize in Physics for "his" many contributions to the field, and in 1933 he emigrated to the United States, escaping Nazi Germany and arriving to a position as a professor of theoretical physics at Princeton University.

Mileva, meanwhile, remained in Switzerland, raising their two sons alone with no professional credit to her name. She suffered a nervous breakdown, and Eduard developed schizophrenia. The medical expenses left Mileva struggling financially; she survived on income from giving private tutoring sessions and irregular alimony from Albert. At one point, she considered revealing her contributions to his work, to which Albert responded in a letter: "You made me laugh when you started threatening me with your recollections. Have you ever considered, even just for a second, that nobody would ever pay attention to your says [*sic*] if the man you talked about had not accomplished something important. When someone is completely insignificant, there is nothing else to say to this person but to remain modest and silent. This is what I advise you to do."

And it is what she did until her death in 1948.

In the late 1950s, Hans-Albert's wife, Frieda, was going to publish letters Mileva and Albert had sent to their sons over the years, but she was swiftly blocked by Albert's estate executors in an attempt to "preserve Einstein's myth." The executors have prevented other publications, too. When some of five hundred letters finally made it to the public eye in 1987, only ten from Mileva to Albert survived, compared to the forty-three sent in the opposite direction. And accordingly, the Einstein myth remains, in many versions of history, as a false fact. It's time this myth was debunked and the truth written into history: the Einstein myth did not result from his genius alone, but from *theirs*.

# Katherine Johnson

***1918–2020***

IN 1961, ALAN SHEPARD BECAME THE FIRST American to travel to space. In 1962, John Glenn became the first American to orbit the earth. And in 1969, Neil Armstrong became the first person to walk on the moon.

Space travel rapidly accelerated starting in the mid-1950s, because the United States was in a space race with the Soviet Union (now Russia). The finish line was sending humans to outer space, and the race was just one part of the Cold War—a battle that broke out between the world's two greatest powers following World War II. The communist USSR thought they had won when they sent the first person in history into space in 1957, with the United States trailing behind and achieving the same feat only in 1961. The USSR proved themselves once again when, a month later in 1961, they successfully launched the first person into orbit around Earth; the United States, again, trailed behind and only achieved the same in 1962. But in 1969, the US took the lead when the first rocket landed on the moon.

In this context, astronauts like Alan, John, and Neil were welcomed back to Earth in the glare of the national spotlight as heroes in the media and history-makers in the books. Behind the scenes, however, at the National Aeronautics and Space Administration (NASA) offices in Virginia, a number of women basked quietly in the glory of having contributed to these groundbreaking achievements. Outside their personal networks, though, these women received no credit—not even Katherine Johnson, the mathematician who calculated by hand the entire trajectories of the rockets that sent men into space, around the earth, and to the moon.

Katherine, born Creola Katherine Coleman in 1918 in West Virginia, was interested in math from a young age. She counted the dishes in the kitchen cupboards, the number of steps on her way to church, and even attempted to count the number of stars in the sky. She couldn't wait to take algebra and geometry, but her town's public education system was segregated and did not have a high school for Black students—it was the middle of the Jim Crow era, a particularly violent, oppressive, segregated part of US history targeting African Americans. So Katherine's family moved to a town 125 miles away, where she and her sisters could continue their education. Katherine began high school at the age of ten, and entered West Virginia Collegiate Institute (later renamed West Virginia State University) when she was only fifteen.

In 1937, Katherine graduated summa cum laude with a double major in mathematics and French, but she found herself facing limited job opportunities. Like most women at the time, she soon married and briefly worked as a teacher—until the moment she saw an opportunity to attend graduate school.

In 1940, Katherine became one of three Black students to integrate the all-white West Virginia University, where she studied advanced mathematics. But when she discovered she was pregnant one year later, she withdrew from the program and returned to domestic life and teaching for more than a decade.



Everything changed in 1952, though, when Katherine learned about NASA and their human computer program: in 1935, NASA's precursor, the National Advisory Committee for Aeronautics (NACA), hired hundreds of white women to join the Langley memorial Aeronautical Laboratory in Virginia as human computers. They were tasked with carrying out mathematics and physics equations by hand—work that was considered mundane and secretarial. Then, during World War II, Langley expanded its human-computer program and began hiring Black women with college degrees.

Katherine applied and was hired in 1953 to tabulate sheets of data for NASA's male engineers at "a time when computers wore skirts," she famously said. Two weeks into the job, she was "borrowed" by the Flight Research Division, where "the guys all had graduate degrees in mathematics," she said, but "they had forgotten all the geometry they ever knew." Katherine, however, remembered her geometry and helped compute the aerodynamic forces on airplanes with ease. She officially transferred to the division as its first and only Black member, and remained there until she retired in 1986.

When the space race began a few years after Katherine started at NASA, the Flight Research Division was tasked with making an American trip to space happen—and it was top secret. So secret, in fact, that sometimes the mathematicians themselves didn't even know what they were doing until they read about it in an aviation journal. But the general assignment was the trajectory of the rockets: "As NASA got ready to put someone in space, they needed to know what the launch conditions were," Katherine recalled. "It was our assignment to develop the launch window and determine where it was going to land."

Katherine loved her job, despite working sixteen-hour days. There wasn't a single day when she woke up and wasn't excited to go to work, for "we were the pioneers of the space era," she said. Her dedication to being a computer helped her cope with personal difficulties, including the loss of her husband in 1956 to brain cancer. Over the years, she published more than twenty-four technical papers, and even became one of the first women to coauthor an official NASA report. In 1959, she was also remarried to a US Army captain and took his last name: Johnson.

At the same time, Katherine was busy making her most memorable contributions to NASA. She calculated, with not much more than a pencil, a slide rule, and graph paper, the trajectories of the Mercury Project mission, which sent the first American into orbit around Earth, and the Apollo 11 mission, which sent the first men to the moon and brought them back safely. Without her, the United States space program never would have left its mark on history—and the USSR would've won the race.

Yet it took almost five decades for her contributions to be recognized.

It wasn't until 2015, only five years before her death, that Katherine was awarded with the Presidential Medal of Freedom by President Barack Obama. And he had, most likely, only learned about her genius from Margot Lee Shetterly's research for her book *Hidden Figures*, which elucidated Katherine's position, alongside those of her peers Mary Jackson and Dorothy Vaughan, as well as catalyzing a scramble to run a new race: that of rewriting NASA's history. Margot had begun working on the book in 2010; its 2016 release was so anticipated that it received a Hollywood treatment that same year. In 2016, Katherine was also, at the age of ninety-eight, presented with the special NASA honor of a Silver Snoopy Award and a NASA Group Achievement award. By 2019, she had been awarded the Congressional Gold Medal, but her history is still being written: NASA has since renamed three facilities in her honor, and in 2021, she was posthumously inducted into the National Women's Hall of Fame.

# Vera Rubin

***1928–2016***

ON A CLEAR, STARRY NIGHT IN 1974, astronomer Vera Rubin made a discovery so revolutionary that it was like humanity learning the earth was round all over again. Vera had evidence proving that everything people thought existed in the universe—stars and planets, light and energy, gas and liquids, rocks, plants, clouds, even humans—composes only 5 percent of what is actually here. She had proven the existence of dark matter: the invisible substance that makes up about 27 percent of the universe.

Vera, who is now known as one of the most important astronomers and astrophysicists in history, was fascinated by the stars and night skies her entire life. When she moved with her family from Philadelphia to Washington, DC, in 1938 at the age of ten, she started drawing maps of the stars and watching meteor showers outside her bedroom window. With the help of her father, she even built her first telescope from cardboard. "By about age twelve, I would prefer to stay up and watch the stars than go to sleep," she said during an interview in 1989. "There was just nothing as interesting in my life as watching the stars every night."

When Vera was coming of age in the late 1940s and early '50s, not only was astronomy a young field of study, but most universities, including those with astronomy departments, did not accept women. Despite this, Vera persisted. She eventually earned an undergraduate degree from Vassar College in 1948 and a graduate degree from Cornell University in 1951, but not without stigmas: she was the only woman, and the only astronomy student, in each department.

The fact that Vera was a woman not only impacted where she could study, but also how seriously her work was taken. While Vera was studying at Cornell, the accepted theory regarding large-scale motions of galaxies was based on the Big Bang Theory, which suggests that the universe is constantly expanding outward. In her master's thesis, Vera presented a new theory: that galaxies were not only expanding outward, but may also be rotating around an unknown center. When she presented her research in December 1950, at just twenty-two years old, to the American Astronomical Society (AAS), they rejected her findings, which were never published. Today, Vera's then-rejected theory is accepted as fact.

Another major breakthrough of Vera's career happened while she was a graduate student at Cornell. While looking for ways to prove the theory in her master's thesis, Vera identified the supergalactic plane, which can be thought of as the equator line running through the galaxy cluster that the Milky Way Galaxy is in. The supergalactic plane was the missing piece that made the science behind her theory of rotating galaxies make sense. At the time, the AAS community was too busy rejecting her thesis to pay attention to this additional discovery. To this day, the credit for this discovery is popularly attributed to Gérard de Vaucouleurs, an older, highly esteemed French astronomer who identified the supergalactic plane three years later, in 1953.

Fast-forward to 1954: while working toward a PhD at Georgetown University, with one child at home and another on the way, Vera discovered that galaxies are clumped together, rather than randomly strewn around space as the scientific community had believed. It was a remarkable discovery that is now part of mainstream astronomy. Yet, once again, the AAS rejected her work, and the knowledge was ignored for twenty years. Not only were her findings ignored by the scientific community at large, but her own institution still didn't allow women into academic offices at the time. Throughout her PhD studies, Vera was forced to meet her mentor in the lobby.

Vera soon began working at the Carnegie Institution's Department of Terrestrial Magnetism, where one of her peers was Kent Ford, a designer of astronomical instruments. Ford had invented the most advanced spectrometer of the time, a tool that measures light coming in from distant corners of the universe, which allowed Vera to study galaxies with unprecedented precision. (Initially, though, she wasn't allowed into the research center to use the telescopes because she was a woman; her eventual permission to enter paved the way for all female astronomers to come.)

At this point, Vera was an expert on galactic dynamics—in other words, the movements of clusters of stars—so she and Kent observed stars' motions to figure out what causes them to move the way they do. They worked closely together for many a starry night, peering through the massive telescopes at the observatory, but their professional roles were very different. "He built the instruments, and I . . . did the science," Vera said in 1989, "but we always observed together because we both liked to."

At the time, astronomers thought that the planets and stars that make up galaxies moved according to the laws of gravity. Stars in the center of the galaxy—a much denser area filled with more stars (i.e., mass)—should move faster than those on the outskirts, which were farther apart, thus having less mass and gravitational force making them move. Mercury, Venus, and Earth, for example, orbit the Sun much faster than planets that are farther away, like Jupiter or Saturn.

Yet by 1974 Vera had observed that the outer stars in other galaxies move much faster than existing science could explain. In comparison to the number of stars they could see, the shapes and movements of these galaxies didn't make any sense. According to the laws of gravity, what Vera first observed in the Andromeda galaxy was impossible: the stars in the outskirts were moving so fast, the whole galaxy should have flown apart.

Vera wanted answers. She was familiar with the concept of dark matter—originally theorized by Jan Oort in 1932 and Fritz Zwicky in 1933—the belief that a "missing mass" must exist in order to create enough gravity to hold fast-moving galaxies together. The astronomical community, however, largely dismissed the missing-mass theory as too far-out to be taken seriously. How could invisible undetectable matter exist?

But Vera witnessed the impossibly quick stars in the outskirts of hundreds of galaxies and eventually concluded that there was no other explanation that could justify the phenomenon she was repeatedly observing. She collected enough evidence to substantiate Jan and Fritz's theory—enough to prove their discovery of dark matter, the invisible matter or "missing mass" that affects not only how galaxies move but also how the universe came to be and what it will become.

Although dark matter to this day has not been observed directly, its existence was confirmed because of the visible effects it has on the matter around it, which scientists *can* see. Proving the existence of dark matter revolutionized humankind's understanding of the universe. Scientists continued building upon Vera's work, and in 1998 another expansion of the universe was discovered: dark energy, an equally mysterious matter that is estimated to make up 68 percent of the universe.

The discoverers of dark energy would go on to earn a Nobel Prize, so it's worth noting that Vera's recognition of dark matter did not. The lack of official acclaim for Vera's discovery and her work with Kent has been heavily contested—after all, it changed the very foundations for our modern understanding of the cosmos.

# Jocelyn Bell Burnell

*1943–*

THE 1960S WERE AMONG THE MOST EXCITING decades in astronomical history. Not only were the first astronauts launched into space—first briefly, then to orbit the earth, and, by 1969, to walk on the moon—but satellites were also being launched. While satellites may not have received as much press coverage as the American astronauts and Soviet cosmonauts, they, along with increasingly advanced telescopes, are what allowed astronomers and astrophysicists to probe space further and more deeply.

In 1965, a young astrophysicist named Jocelyn Bell Burnell began her doctorate studies at Cambridge University. She spent two years stringing together thousands of antennas and wiring 120 miles of cables, working alongside a handful of other postgraduate students to build a new radio telescope designed by their professor, the astrophysicist Anthony "Tony" Hewish. Tony's telescope was an integral tool for the team as they researched emissions from space, part of which included searching for quasars—the light that is emitted from supermassive black holes. With this new telescope, they would be able to detect very, very distant objects in space by recording radio wavelengths.

But it was only after construction that the real work—chart analysis—began. And on August 6, 1967, after only a few weeks spent analyzing data sets that took up almost a hundred feet of paper per day, Jocelyn noticed a curious signal in the data that neither she nor any established science at the time could explain. It was not a quasar, for the marks in question were fast and regular, and she had never seen anything like them. She called Tony to tell him about the quarter-inch blip in the long, continuous lines of information, but he dismissed the find as a fluke caused by Jocelyn wrongly wiring the telescope. Jocelyn knew she had not wired the telescope incorrectly, so she kept running tests, only to see that the first blip was not a one-off occurrence. *Blip . . . blip . . . blip. . . .* She was now looking at a string of pulses happening 1.33 seconds apart.

She again called Tony, who again dismissed it as a technical interference. "I knew it wasn't interference," asserted Jocelyn.

Eventually, after enough calls, Tony accepted the fact that Jocelyn had found something worth exploring. At first, Tony and Jocelyn ideated together. They jokingly named the pulses "LGM," short for "Little Green Men," indicating that they might be signals from aliens. But one day,

Jocelyn walked in on Tony and Martin Ryle—the head of the Cambridge radio astronomy group and director of the Mullard Radio Astronomy Observatory, where they were conducting their research—having a meeting. She sensed she was being wrongfully left out of what seemed to be an important discussion, yet she remained committed to the project and soon found three more strings of pulses in the data, all from different parts of space. Now Jocelyn had compiled enough evidence to present her findings, even if she and Tony weren't yet sure exactly what they might mean.



On February 24, 1968, Jocelyn and Tony published their research in an article titled "Observation of a Rapidly Pulsating Radio Source" in the journal *Nature*, along with three other coauthors: John Pilkington, Paul Scott, and R. A. Collins. A few days before the journal was issued publicly, though, Tony announced Jocelyn's findings at a private lecture at Cambridge University. It was a full house, and Fred Hoyle, one of the most esteemed astronomers of the 20th century and a personal hero of Jocelyn's, was in attendance. Tony barely mentioned Jocelyn in the presentation ("[he] could've cited me more and didn't," Jocelyn reflected in an interview for the *New York Times* in 2021), and, by the end, Fred had solved the mystery as to what the pulses were indicating.

His explanation, which turned out to be correct, was that the pulses resulted from supernova remnants: the blips Jocelyn had detected in the data were beams of radiation coming out of fast-spinning, super-dense neutron stars. In other words, they indicated pulsating electromagnetic radiation—or, more simply, radio pulsars.

But, as Jocelyn had discovered, neutron stars emit more than just undetectably faint light: they emit detectable radio waves. And, when positioned just right, the rotating star will sweep a radio wave past Earth, much like the spotlight of a lighthouse.

A few months later, on May 25, 1968, when astrophysicist Thomas Gold published his paper "Rotating Neutron Stars as the Origin of the Pulsating Radio Sources" in *Nature*, it became widely accepted that the pulsars were precisely what Fred had predicted at the Cambridge lecture. Tony also published his own explanation for what the pulsating radio sources could be that same year in *Scientific American*, but his theory was quickly disproven.

The discovery of radio pulsars, and the early idea that they *might* be extraterrestrial life, captured the media's attention, and Jocelyn and her team experienced a deluge of press. In the 2021 *New York Times* interview, Jocelyn recalled how reporters would ask Tony science questions and then turn to her for what they called "human interest," posing questions like whether she would describe herself as brunette or blond, or how many boyfriends she had. They even went so far as to ask what her bust, waist, and hip measurements were. "I barely rated as a scientist," she explained. "Tony just let it happen, it was dreadful."

But the real punch in the gut came in 1974, when Tony and Martin Ryle received the Nobel Prize in Physics "for their pioneering research in radio astrophysics." While Tony's inclusion in the award was of course deserved (he had, after all, designed the radio telescope, developed the radio research curriculum he and Jocelyn worked on, and raised the money to build the telescope and pursue the research), Jocelyn deserved recognition too: she had run the telescope, analyzed the data, and single-handedly discovered the first four pulsars—not to mention the fact that she had fought for them to be studied further. It was surely a team of two, but only one of the two was fairly awarded.

Today, the discovery of radio pulsars is considered one of the most groundbreaking achievements in modern astrophysics. As astrophysicist Iosif Shklovsky told Jocelyn in 1970, she had "made the greatest astronomical discovery of the twentieth century." Because neutron stars rotate at a stable pace, and the timing of pulses is precise and predictable, scientists now use pulsars to measure vast cosmic distances, search for planets in faraway solar systems, and study some of the densest, most mysterious phenomena in space. In 1993, the discovery of binary pulsars—two pulsars stuck in orbit around each other—even earned another Nobel Prize, awarded to astrophysicists Joseph Taylor and Russell Hulse. And more recently, pulsars have become vital tools in the study of gravity, such as measuring how heavy objects in space curve the space-time continuum.

Though she was left out of the Nobel's accolades, finally, in 2018, Jocelyn was awarded the Breakthrough Prize—a global science award founded in 2012—for her long-ago discovery. She promptly donated the award of $3 million to the Institute of Physics, with the explicit instruction to create research scholarships exclusively for minorities and women. She may not have had a role model to look up to when she herself was young, but with her legacy, Jocelyn is ensuring that future women astrophysicists do.

# Dropping the Bomb—on Science

*Women were behind the life-altering scientific breakthroughs that led to the development of the atomic bomb and nuclear energy*



Until the United States dropped atomic bombs on the Japanese cities of Hiroshima and Nagasaki on August 6 and 9, 1945, no one had ever before witnessed a weapon of mass destruction of such magnitude. Over a hundred thousand people were killed, and the long-term effects of the toxic radiation have affected the health of people in those regions ever since. From that day forward, nuclear power altered the possibilities of war—and the fear that war instills.

But the bombings of Hiroshima and Nagasaki were not the first time nuclear weapons had been detonated. The United States, Great Britain, and other Allied Powers during World War II had been in a race against time to invent a working atomic weapon as soon as the nuclear physicist Lise Meitner and her collaborators

Otto Robert Frisch, Otto Hahn, and Fritz Strassmann discovered nuclear fission in 1938. Their discovery opened the floodgates: scientists on both sides of the war were rushed into learning how to harness the incomprehensible power that results from breaking an atom's nucleus in half.

In the US, this led to a top-secret endeavor called the Manhattan Project. Scientists were herded to clandestine labs around the country, the largest of which was in Los Alamos, New Mexico, where they worked to develop a weapon of mass destruction.

But when Lise Meitner made her groundbreaking discovery and Chien-Shiung Wu was recruited for the Manhattan Project, neither woman knew what was to come—and neither did the men who received the Nobel Prizes for the work.

However, Lise's and Chien-Shiung's contributions to the development of nuclear science were not all about detrimental detonation. The work of these women and countless others has led to advancements in nuclear energy as a peaceful electric-power source, as well as broadening our understanding of the inner workings of the universe.

Lise Meitner
1878–1968

ON THE MORNING OF CHRISTMAS EVE, 1938, nuclear physicist Lise Meitner strolled through the snow in Kungalv, Sweden, with her nephew Otto Robert Frisch, a fellow nuclear physicist. Lise wanted to consult him about a letter she'd received from her long-time collaborator, the chemist Otto Hahn, that outlined the startling results of a nuclear experiment. In it, Hahn explained that he had bombarded an atom of uranium with neutrons, and in the aftermath, there was no trace of the element radium, as he and his team had expected to see; instead, there was barium. Little did they know they had just ignited the launch of the nuclear age.

Lise and Otto Hahn had worked together for decades in Berlin, Germany, until Lise, who was Jewish, was forced to flee in 1938 as the Nazi party rose to power. The pair first met in 1907, when Lise moved to Berlin to work under the renowned physicist Max Planck, who had only agreed to give her a postdoctoral position under one condition: she was to work for free, and only in back-room labs or the cellar.

But Lise was committed to nuclear physics, and these stipulations did not deter her. She had, after all, already surmounted countless battles as a woman. Lise was born in Austria in 1878 and excelled in primary school, but women at the time were not allowed to attend high school or gain a higher education. Luckily, her family was affluent, and her parents encouraged her interests, so they hired private tutors to continue her education at home. Then, in 1897, Austria began allowing women to attend universities. In 1901, Lise proved that her private education was adequate and enrolled as one of the very first women at the University of Vienna to study physics. By 1905, she had earned her PhD.

Once in Berlin, Lise thrived despite the limitations. She worked steadfastly under Max and alongside Otto Hahn to study nuclear activity—then a new, little-understood topic. The idea that matter is made of atoms had been scientifically accepted since 1808, but the first near-accurate model of what an atom and its core, the nucleus, might look like had only been proposed in 1911. According to the model, the nucleus of an atom was made of two kinds of subatomic particles (positively charged protons and negatively charged electrons), and the nucleus was believed to be a solid lump that could be altered only in very minor ways; it was not considered something that could be split apart.

With this entirely new world of atomic particles to explore, Lise and Otto were among hundreds of scientists hungry to know more. And as two of the leading scientists in the world conducting atomic research, they made a great team—as a chemist, Otto would execute nuclear experiments that they developed together, and as a physicist, Lise would interpret the results.

In 1917, the pair discovered protactinium, element no. 91 in the periodic table. That same year, Ernest Rutherford observed the first nuclear reaction. He bombarded protons and electrons into a nitrogen atom at high speed, transforming the nitrogen into oxygen. With this, he established two new rules of nuclear physics: firstly, that atoms can decay or transform into another element; and secondly, that radiation, or energy, is emitted from the atom's nucleus during the process of decay.

Building on this, in 1922 Lise discovered a process in which an atom with an electron vacancy will re-stabilize by ejecting one or more additional electrons. But the following year, French scientist Pierre Auger independently came across the same thing and is credited for the discovery, with the process today being known as the "Auger Effect."



Then, in 1932, the English physicist James Chadwick changed the nuclear landscape once again when he discovered neutrons: a third, uncharged (neutral) subatomic particle in an atom's nucleus. With neutrons now in the nuclear equation, scientists theorized that if uncharged neutrons—instead of charged protons and electrons—were used to bombard the nucleus of an atom, they could more easily collide with the atom, thereby causing a nuclear reaction and transforming atoms into new elements.

As Lise and Otto continued to conduct research, the Nazis' fascist ideology was on the rise outside the university. By the late 1930s, anti-semitism had seeped into every corner of Germany. Violence against Jewish people increased at an alarming rate, and new laws began to bar German Jews from holding jobs and positions at universities. Lise, who was Jewish but an Austrian citizen, was not immediately affected, but when Germany invaded and annexed Austria in March 1938, it invalidated her Austrian passport. She didn't want to leave, but Otto feared for her life: with the help of a Dutch colleague, Lise narrowly escaped to the Netherlands, carrying ten marks (today, about fifty dollars) and a hidden diamond ring. She left everything else behind.

Once Lise settled in Sweden, she and Otto continued collaborating across borders. So, when he was utterly puzzled by the appearance of barium during a chemical experiment, he immediately wrote to Lise, relying on her to make sense of it. And on Christmas Eve 1938, on that snowy stroll through the Swedish forest with her nephew, she did.

Otto and his assistant Fritz Strassman had bombarded uranium with a neutron. When barium—an element only about half the size of uranium—resulted, they were bewildered. Ernest Rutherford had proven atoms can decay and transform, but nothing of such a drastic difference had ever been observed. Upon repeating the test, Otto, Fritz, and Lise proved that it wasn't a mistake, and, using her nephew's mind as a springboard, Lise concluded that the uranium nucleus had split in half.

If she based her calculations on a theory of the atomic nucleus posed by the Danish physicist Niels Bohr in 1936, it was possible that a neutron impacting a large, unstable nucleus could in fact cause the nucleus to not only decay but to break.

Moreover, she calculated that the breaking of a nucleus could release a thousand times more energy than any other chemical reaction ever recorded. Lise's nephew, borrowing a biological term indicating the instant when a replicating cell splits into two, named the process nuclear fission.

News of their discovery spread quickly. Within weeks, it was discovered that the fission of a highly radioactive version of a uranium atom (uranium's 235 isotope) would release even more neutrons when impacted, thus releasing an even more powerful chain reaction and resulting in larger quantities of radioactive energy.

Lise and her nephew knew the significance of the atomic discovery that she had made, and what the subsequent realization about the 235 isotope meant: it would enable humans to unleash a burst of radioactive energy rivaling a thousand tons of explosive TNT through only a few ounces' worth of microscopic chemical reactions. With Adolf Hitler in power and the world teetering on the brink of what became World War II, Lise did not want this information made public. But the discovery was too big to be kept secret.

Otto Hahn and Fritz published an article in *Naturwissenschaften* in January 1939. The following month, Lise and Otto Frisch published a physics-backed explanation of the experiment's results in *Nature*.

Lise refused any involvement with making a weapon based on nuclear fission, but that didn't stop others. Word of the experiment spread to Leo Szilárd and then to Albert Einstein, who, fearing it would not be long before Nazi Germany developed their own nuclear weapon, wrote a desperate letter to President Roosevelt, voicing concern over what might happen if Germany got ahold of uranium stores and developed a bomb first. Ultimately, it turned out that Germany was never even close to developing one; when the Americans succeeded in doing so, Leo, Albert, and Lise all staunchly opposed its use. But the US government had other plans.

And then, in 1944, Otto Hahn alone received the Nobel Prize in Chemistry for the revolutionary discovery of nuclear fission, despite Lise's integral role in unlocking the meaning of his experiment's secret, not to mention the fact that her nephew came up with the process's name. Otto Hahn became an acclaimed public figure, renowned as a Nobel laureate, "a decent German who never gave in to the Nazis," and a scientist who, thankfully, didn't build a bomb. In 1966, in an effort to partly rectify Lise's exclusion from the Nobel Prize, the US Department of Energy jointly awarded her, Otto Hahn, and Fritz Strassmann the US Fermi Prize. But when Lise died in 1968, aged eighty-nine, her trusted collaborator had not once mentioned her critically groundbreaking analysis of the uranium experiment, her contributions to the team in Berlin, or their ongoing work together after she had been exiled, in any of his countless articles, interviews, memoirs, or autobiographies.

# Chien-Shiung Wu

*1912–1997*

WHEN THE UNITED STATES DROPPED TWO atomic bombs over Japan on August 6 and 9, 1945, it effectively ended World War II, but also over 100,000 lives. The scientists who had developed the bomb were some of the most intelligent people of the 20th century, and they had been recruited by the US government to work on a top-secret initiative: the Manhattan Project. With clandestine labs scattered across the country, many of the project's contributors had no idea that their careers would culminate in the creation of an unfathomably powerful weapon of mass destruction.

One of these scientists was Chien-Shiung Wu, without whom the development of the atomic bomb might have never happened. She was a leading nuclear physicist and a vital mind to the Manhattan Project; throughout her career, she made countless discoveries and contributions that forever changed the field.

Chien-Shiung was born in 1912, in Liuhe, China, about thirty miles from Shanghai. A year before her birth, the Republic of China had been established, and with it came a new generation of leaders who wanted to change the status quo, including society's attitude toward women. One of those leaders was Chien-Shiung's father, Zhongyi Wu, who believed in equal rights for women in an era when Chinese girls were still expected to bind their feet and uphold a subservient place in society. Few girls were formally educated at the time, but Zhongyi wanted a different life for his daughter, so he and his wife founded the Mingde School for Girls.

The Mingde School only taught students through the fourth grade, so in 1922, at the age of ten, Chien-Shiung was sent to a boarding school. For the next seven years, she worked tirelessly to gain the skills required to study physics at China's National Central University. Her dedication paid off, and in 1930 she enrolled. Four years later, she graduated at the top of her class. But when Chien-Shiung began postgraduate work at Zhejiang University, she hit a wall: no Chinese university had a program for the growing field of nuclear physics, which she wanted to pursue. Encouraged by a mentor to complete her PhD in the United States, and supported financially by her uncle, Chien-Shiung boarded a ship to San Francisco, in 1936.

Upon arrival, Chien-Shiung threw herself into research at the University of California, Berkeley, which was quickly becoming the global epicenter for studying the atom. She developed an expertise in an area of radioactivity called beta decay, a type of radioactive disintegration, or what occurs when an unstable atom ejects bits of itself to become stable again. In the process of beta decay, the atom emits nuclear energy and transforms into other elements. Her research took on a new level when, in 1938, Lise Meitner and her collaborators discovered nuclear fission—the ability of the nucleus of an atom to not just change form, but to split in half.

With this groundbreaking discovery, Chien-Shiung forged ahead as the field of nuclear physics progressed. By 1940, she had earned her PhD, as well as a reputation as an authority on nuclear fission, beta decay, and atomic science as a whole. She even helped solve a critical issue in what was to be the world's first nuclear reactor, laying the foundations for the production of nuclear energy.

Her brilliance, however, was not enough to earn her a full-time job at Berkeley. Plus, sexism in science paired with growing anti-Asian attitudes on the West Coast as the US entered World War II resulted in scarce job offers on a more general level. So, when her husband, another scientist, was offered a position on the East Coast in 1942, she accompanied him. Here, she found a teaching position at Smith College, but the school lacked research facilities, so in 1943 she began working at Princeton—a position she was offered primarily because there was a shortage of men, who had been sent to fight in World War II. After all, Princeton at the time did not allow women to attend, let alone teach. Chien-Shiung thus became Princeton's first-ever female faculty member, even though women would not be allowed to enroll for another twenty-six years.

By this time, nuclear physics was as unstable as the atoms that scientists were studying—new, colossal atomic advancements and discoveries were being published at an incredibly rapid rate. Before long, the US government, afraid that Nazi Germany might harness the power of a splitting atom into a weapon first, recruited Chien-Shiung, along with many former professors and colleagues from Berkeley, to form the Manhattan Project.

One of a handful of women to be working in the project's top levels, and the only Chinese person in the project at all, Chien-Shiung's expertise was invaluable. Her recent research had focused on transforming the most common type of uranium, which is not fissionable, into a rarer type that is. For the next two years, she conducted experiments trying to solve this mystery, which was the center of the Manhattan Project; solving it would provide the fuel for the atomic bomb.

When the project succeeded, many lives were lost, but it also marked the end of the war. Chien-Shiung jumped right back into her research on beta decay, and in 1945 she was given a research position at Columbia University. Determined to prove a theory posed in 1933, she devised an experiment that showed exactly how beta decay works, or how some radioactive atoms can stabilize themselves and become less radioactive while doing so.

Providing the experimental data to prove the 1933 beta-decay theory was Chien-Shiung's third major breakthrough in the field of nuclear physics—and about a decade later, in 1956, she made a fourth when she disproved the law of conservation of parity.

Until then, it was believed that nature did not play favorites: that maintaining parity (or a type of symmetry) governed every natural process. In other words, if you watch a clock ticking in a clockwise direction, then look at the clock in a mirror, you will see the clock ticking in exactly the same way but counter-clockwise; the coordinate plane has been flipped, but the physics stay the same. This belief was a fundamental law of science, much like the law of gravity. But what if you looked at the clock in the mirror, and it was still ticking clockwise? Other theoretical physicists had broached the idea that parity may be up for debate, but the scientific community at large thought it so impossible that it was never taken seriously. Then, in 1956, physicists Tsung Dao Lee and Chen Ning Yang theorized that parity was not always conserved in beta-decay nuclear reactions, and they turned to Chien-Shiung for help.

Chien-Shiung canceled what would have been her first trip back to China since she had moved to the US twenty years earlier and went to work. After six months of preparation, the experiment was ready to be performed. Two days after Christmas, 1956, in the extreme conditions Chien-Shiung had developed for this test, she and her team carefully observed the nucleus of a cobalt atom during beta decay. If the law of conservation of parity had been upheld, the expelled electrons would have flown symmetrically in both directions. But they didn't. The results were crystal-clear, in that parity was not conserved. Nature, it turns out, does sometimes play favorites.

Chien-Shiung, Tsung Dao, and Chen Ning had disproved a fundamental "fact" of science—an achievement so big that Tsung Dao and Chen Ning received the Nobel Prize in Physics in 1957. Chien-Shiung's name, however, was nowhere to be found.

Chien-Shiung's contributions to the field of nuclear physics were undoubtedly remembered, and she received numerous awards in her lifetime, including the US National Medal of Science in 1975. She was also selected as Italy's Woman of the Year in 1981 and inducted into the United States' National Women's Hall of Fame in 1998. In 1990, she even became the first living scientist to have an asteroid named after her: Asteroid 2752 Wu Chien-Shiung. But when she died in 1997, the fact remained that she had been left out of the world's most prestigious prize—and the men with whom she had tirelessly worked had received all the credit.

# Women Don't Just Give Life: They Save It

*From debunking the idea that women should experience as much pain as possible during childbirth to discovering antibiotics that would prevent millions of deaths, women have been the backbone of modern biology and reproductive medicine for centuries*



These are two fundamental truths: women give life, and the only certainty in life is death. What has been less certain historically, however, is women's role in curbing the latter.

For all of human history prior to the 1800s, death came early and often. The average person's life expectancy was only around thirty years. People lived fast and died young, and this was primarily due to infection and disease. The onset of the 19th century saw advancements in technology, industry, and civil engineering, and improvements in sanitation, all of which alleviated many common and fatal environmental factors. But it wasn't until the 20th century that many deaths became easily preventable with the discovery of antibiotics.

In the blink of an eye, half of all children under the age of five were no longer expected to die of disease. Hundreds of thousands of soldiers during wartime would be saved from death caused by infection. Blood infections, which could manifest from an incident as large as a miscarriage or as small as a scratch, no longer meant certain death.

While Alexander Fleming was the first to identify penicillin in 1928—which would become the world's first antibiotic—what he discovered could not be produced in large-enough quantities to have any effect. It was not until 1943, when Mary Hunt found a new mold, that enough penicillin could be produced to save the world. That same year, Elizabeth Bugie helped discover streptomycin, the world's second antibiotic, and the one that would cure tuberculosis. Then there was Esther Lederberg, who made multiple discoveries that would broaden our understanding of bacteria—ergo, infection—and would unearth the basic principles of what would become molecular biology. But as newspapers excitedly reported about these new miracle drugs and discoveries, the stories of these women scientists were buried and their male counterparts rewarded.

The achievements made by Mary, Elizabeth, and Esther are backdropped by the first truth: that women give life. It is women who become pregnant, women who give birth, and women who have been caring for women since the dawn of time. But, like the stories of the 20th-century biologists, the history of Western institutionalized female reproductive medicine is complex. So complex, in fact, that the work and very existence of the world's first gynecologist (that is, the first recorded female doctor of obstetrics in the institution of Western medicine), Trota of Salerno, who revolutionized the practice of women's medicine in the 11th or 12th century, has been entirely contested by male scholars.

# Trota of Salerno

*11th or 12th century*

FOR CENTURIES THROUGHOUT EUROPE, A woman referred to by the name Trota of Salerno was lauded as a pioneering gynecologist and author of *Trotula Major on Gynecology*, also known as *Passionibus mulierum curandorum*, or, in English, *The Diseases of Women*. In the Latin book's three sections and sixty-three chapters, she debunked common theories relating to women's health of the time, including the idea that women should experience as much pain as possible during childbirth as punishment for the sin of the biblical figure of Eve, as well as the belief that it was impossible for men to be infertile. She advocated for women's health, such as for the use of opiates during labor to ease pain, and suggested that men can in fact be sterile.

Her legacy, in the form of the book, spread throughout the medieval medical world for years after her death. Over the centuries, the book was translated from Latin into many other languages—including English, French, German, Flemish, and Catalan—and doctors around the world hailed her work. The British author, poet, and civil servant Geoffrey Chaucer—commonly referred to as the "father of English literature"—even referenced her in the prologue to his iconic collection *The Canterbury Tales*, first published in the 14th century. Furthermore, her work was even cited by authoritative medical writers of the time, including Peter of Spain, also known as Pope John XXI.

But this all changed in 1566, when Hans Kaspar Wolf published a new edition of Trota's work, listing the author as Eros Juliae, a Roman freedman from the 1st century CE. He also edited the grammar from the masculine to the feminine, to align with the change of name. With these amendments, Hans put into question not only the authenticity of Trota's work and her gender, but also her entire existence.

Hans's new attribution was based on unsupported nonsense, yet it lit a fire that could be easily fueled, as few concrete facts were recorded about Trota's life in southern Italy. She may have belonged to the wealthy di Ruggiero family, or married the physician Johannes Platearius and had two sons. However, it is commonly accepted that Trota did indeed exist and that she attended and likely taught at what is believed to be the Western world's first medical school, the School of Salerno. Believing this, many authors like to refer to her as the world's first female professor of medicine and first female gynecologist—with regard to institutionalized, Western medicine. (What's more, not only is there evidence that many women attended the institution in the 11th and 12th centuries, but the school was also the most important source of medical knowledge in Western Europe at the time, as the pivotal center for the influx of Arabic medical treatises and Greek texts.)

The fire lit by Hans was also fueled by shifting dynamics in medicine. Around the same time as the publication of his edition, the fields of gynecology and medicine in the West were changing from a skill to a profession linked to academic training, degrees, and licenses. Women still filled the roles of midwives and attendants during births, but the wealthier families increasingly sought guidance and healthcare from academically trained physicians—and since women were barred from university educations at the time, this meant they were also excluded from the formal field of medicine. Universities soon became the regulators of Western medical fields, and then female midwives, attendants, healers, and other "unlicensed" practitioners could be prosecuted as charlatans. Thus, in the centuries following Trota's life, women's health was thrust fully into the hands of men, where it primarily still lies today.



So, from the point of view of Hans's 16th-century edition until today, Trota has existed as a contested figure. Some scholars express doubt that she was a woman; others believe she was an entirely fictional character. Some conjecture that a male physician named Trottus wrote the book and that Trotula was just a midwife. Though many (primarily male) scholars continue to argue against her existence, or at least against her authorship of *The Diseases of Women*, feminist scholars are convinced of her life and work, especially due to the name of the book. The word "Trotula" is the diminutive form of "Trota," meaning "the little [work of] Trota." (Due to this, Trota is also commonly referred to as Trotula of Salerno.) A trot was a woman who trotted for a living, who was too old to be considered attractive, and who, in her business, taught tricks, tips, and lessons about women's sexual pleasure. In *The Diseases of Women*, Trota gave medical advice concerning conception, menstruation, pregnancy, and childbirth, but also beauty aids, toothpowders and pastes, hair-removal techniques, and treatments for body odor.

Trota's ideas were revolutionary, whether she lived during the 1000s or 1100s, and her medical practices were previously unheard of. In addition to *The Diseases of Women*, she also authored the *Practica secundum Trotam* (*Practical Medicine According to Trota*), a book of practical medicine that demonstrated her broad scope of knowledge. In it, she writes about a variety of topics, from infertility and menstrual disorders to snake bites and cosmetics.

Her methods paved the way for the development of obstetrics and gynecology, with *The Diseases of Women* still regarded as the definitive sourcebook for pre-modern medical practices. Yet as soon as Hans made the claim that Trota had not existed, or at the very least had not written even a portion of the three-part book, the male-dominated medical community was quick to adopt and expand on his theory. Trota may have been given a seat at the table in artist Judy Chicago's iconic feminist installation *The Dinner Party* (1979), but her proper place in history books remains a point of contention.

# Mary Hunt

***1943–unknown***

IN THE LATE 1920S, THE SCOTTISH MICRO-biologist Alexander Fleming discovered that chemicals produced by mold could kill infection-causing bacteria. The mold was *penicillium notatum*, so he named the chemical "penicillin"—one of today's most common antibiotics.

Yet Alexander could not figure out how to extract enough penicillin from the mold for it to be an effective treatment on humans. Building on his research in 1939, chemists Ernst Chain and Sir Howard Florey, along with their assistant Norman Heatley, managed to distill concentrated penicillin from the mold, but it was terribly difficult and took weeks to produce a single dose. Time and time again, the delicate mold would dissolve during the extraction process. During clinical trials, for example, Anne Miller, a patient suffering from streptococcal infection, a common cause of death back then, was cured after receiving a tablespoon of penicillin in 1942.

But, to put things in perspective, that sacred tablespoon was half of the entire amount of the antibiotic available in the United States. To complete Anne's treatment after that initial tablespoon, doctors collected her urine, extracted the unabsorbed penicillin, and then reinjected it into her body.

Parallel to their research, Europe was falling deeper and deeper into World War II, adding a moral pressure to their quest: the scientists knew that in World War I, around half of the ten million soldiers who died perished not from the attacks of warfare itself but from untreatable infections caused by relatively minor wounds and injuries. With penicillin, they could prevent such deaths. England, however, was overburdened with wartime demands and had limited supplies. Thus, Howard looked to the United States for help, specifically to the Rockefeller Foundation. In July 1941, he and Norman arrived in New York: they would teach American researchers how to produce penicillin molds in exchange for a kilogram (2.205 pounds) of the drug. During their trip, they traveled to the Department of Agriculture's Northern Regional Research Laboratory in Peoria, Illinois, establishing what would become America's most important penicillin lab.

When Pearl Harbor was attacked in December 1941 and the United States found itself part of the war, the domestic need for the drug skyrocketed. And as the war escalated throughout 1942, scientist Andrew Moyer led the lab in Peoria, desperate to find a potent penicillin mold that would not disintegrate during the extraction

process and that would produce more penicillin than *penicillium notatum*. It is here that a little-known assistant held a pivotal role.

Mary Hunt worked at Andrew's lab. Every day, she scoured local markets for decaying fruit or any fresh foods with fungal growth. One day in 1943, she saw a cantaloupe forming a mold on its navel at the grocery store. She brought it back to the lab, where she cut off the mold and prepared it for research, passing the remaining fruit along to her colleagues. "They thought it tasted very sweet, and they loved the color," she recalled. Andrew took the sample and discovered that it was infected with *penicillium chrysogenum*. Alone, this mold produced two hundred times the amount of penicillin that *penicillium notatum* did. When it was zapped with X-rays to cause mutation, the mutated mold produced over a thousand times the amount of penicillin as had the mold discovered by Alexander.

The news of this discovery spread worldwide, and labs quickly began mass-producing penicillin. Fourteen thousand pounds of the drug were produced to treat battlefield wounds and infections; and in 1945, Alexander, Ernst, and Howard received the Nobel Prize in Physiology or Medicine for their initial discovery of penicillin. Moreover, Ernst and Howard's assistant Norman, as well as Andrew and his lab in Peoria, are well documented and credited in the history of this groundbreaking scientific journey. The role, however, of Mary—a critical assistant without whom the future of penicillin would have taken a completely different course—is largely unaccounted for in the narrative of the drug's history.

It is natural that neither she nor Andrew received the Nobel Prize, but while Andrew's name is celebrated along with those of Alexander, Ernst, Howard, and even Norman, hardly any information about Mary has survived. To this day, scholars do not know when she was born, when she died, or what she may have done beyond finding a moldy cantaloupe in a grocery store. The only known fact is the demeaning nickname she was given by her male colleagues after finding the fruit that changed the course of medical history: Moldy Mary.

# Elizabeth Bugie Gregory

***1920–2001***

ALTHOUGH ANTIBIOTICS ARE NORMAL today, it was only a hundred years ago that they were first discovered. Prior to the development of antibiotics, any wound, no matter how minor, could turn fatal from infection. Suffice it to say that antibiotics are taken for granted in treating ailments and infections in modern medicine, but when these life-saving drugs were first introduced to the public in the early 20th century, it was like medical magic.

The initial breakthrough was the discovery of penicillin in 1928, but at that time scientists did not yet fully understand the drug, and it was extremely difficult to produce. Just a decade later, as the world sank into World War II, scientists continued to exert tremendous efforts to find alternative treatments. In 1943, the world's second-ever antibiotic was discovered: streptomycin.

Streptomycin differed from penicillin in that it was effective against tuberculosis. As one of the leading causes of death around the world, finding a cure for tuberculosis was important; but with the world at war—and soldier casualties resulting from disease matching those from combat—finding as many cures to as many wartime diseases as possible turned the world of biochemistry into an antibiotics race. If a moldy cantaloupe could eventually catalyze the mass production of penicillin—immediately saving thousands, if not millions, of lives—the possibilities for biomedical intervention of infectious diseases seemed endless.

Streptomycin was first isolated and tested by soil scientist Selman Waksman and his team of students at Rutgers University, who knew from their initial testing that the drug had active effects against certain pathogens. However, Selman also knew that the Rutgers University laboratory was not equipped to take the research further: it needed to be tested *in vivo*, on living animals. In 1939, Selman had made an agreement with the giant pharmaceutical company Merck Corporation. In exchange for a grant to study antibiotics and additional funding for promising discoveries, Selman would assign Merck Corporation all patents that came from his research. And if any of the patents proved successful, Merck would pay the Rutgers Foundation a small royalty. So, when it was time to take streptomycin research to the next level, Selman contacted a team of medical researchers at the Mayo Clinic, who agreed to take on the task in March 1944, albeit funded by Merck.

The Mayo Clinic tests were a success. Streptomycin was not only the first nontoxic, effective chemotherapeutic treatment for tuberculosis, but it also was discovered to effectively treat other common diseases, including cholera, urinary tract infections, tularemia, bubonic plague, typhoid fever, and more. Later, in 1944, Selman published "Proceedings of the Society for Experimental and Biological Medicine," a paper detailing the discovery of streptomycin with two co-authors: the first name listed on the paper was that of doctoral student Albert Schatz, followed by a graduate student, Elizabeth Bugie, and, finally, Selman's own. Both Albert and Elizabeth were working in Selman's lab, and, as the list of authors on the published finding suggests, both of them were involved in the discovery of the antibiotic.



However, when Selman and Albert patented streptomycin in February 1945, Elizabeth's name was absent from the application. And once its effectiveness against tuberculosis was officially proven by August 1945, Selman dropped both of his mentees' names from the discussion entirely. He published a paper on his own, and, as the drug had become hugely profitable, he renegotiated his contract with Merck Corporation. The pharmaceutical company agreed to assign patent rights to Rutgers University in exchange for a nonexclusive license for the production of the drug, as well as a royalty rebate to compensate for their investment in the drug's research.

In outrage, Albert sued Selman and the Rutgers Research and Endowment Foundation in March 1950 to be credited as codiscoverer and to receive royalties, in what became a very public case. The suit was eventually settled, with Rutgers receiving 80 percent of the royalties, Selman receiving 10 percent, Albert three, and the remaining seven divided among fourteen others who had been working in the lab, including Elizabeth, who received 0.2 percent. Yet still, Elizabeth's name and role, clearly established by her name's presence on that initial paper, remained in the shadows.

What's more, further controversy surrounded Albert's claim to a stake in this profitable discovery. Albert had only been working on streptomycin in Selman's laboratory for three months before it was deemed ready for live experimentation at the Mayo Clinic. So, while Albert "was concerned with some of the early isolations and tests," as Selman wrote in 1950, "Miss Elizabeth Bugie [has] made as important contributions, if not more so, in the discovery and development of streptomycin than Schatz has done."

Elizabeth was an accomplished microbiologist, who benefited when universities and labs began accepting more female scientists during World War II due to the lack of literal "manpower." After completing her undergraduate studies at the New Jersey College for Women (today known as Douglass Residential College), she earned her master's degree at Rutgers University while working in Selman's lab. Here, before joining the streptomycin project, her research was focused on two other recently found fungal metabolites (chemical substances created by fungi, many of which have been discovered to have antibiotic, antiviral, and other pharmacological properties; penicillin and streptomycin are among them). She had also gone on to study antibiotics to work against plant pathogens, such as the tree-killing fungus that causes Dutch elm disease. Elizabeth's fungal focus of study was unusual at the time, as most research was focused on animal diseases. All of this led to Selman's request for her to work alongside Albert in the search for antibiotics, once the scientific community learned that antimicrobial substances come from fungi.

Almost a decade later, in 1952, Selman alone received the Nobel Prize in Physiology or Medicine for the discovery of streptomycin. By then, Elizabeth had married another microbiologist, Francis Joseph Gregory, and had turned to what women were expected to do at the time: raising a family. She later returned to graduate school in library sciences, but upon her death in 2001, one of her daughters, Patricia Camp, recalled a poignant story: Elizabeth had told her two daughters multiple times about how, when it was time to patent streptomycin, her male colleagues had insisted that it was unimportant for her name to be on the patent, because she "would get married and have a family" and it wouldn't matter. Of course, once the patent was approved without her name, these men propelled a different story, one that only ever acknowledged her as a lowly lab assistant whose work was to confirm their results. Had their version of the story truly been the case, however, her name would have never been on the paper announcing its discovery and she would never have received any amount of royalties, no matter how small. As Patricia recalled Elizabeth saying, "If women's lib had been around, my name would have been on the patent."

# Esther Lederberg

*1922–2006*

WEARING A PROM DRESS AND HAND-DYED slippers at a gala in Stockholm, Esther Zimmer Lederberg watched as her then-husband accepted a Nobel Prize in Physiology or Medicine—an award given to him in 1958 for a discovery in which her own research had played an essential role. Esther and Joshua Lederberg had worked in microbiological research as a husband-and-wife team for over a decade. Together they published scientific papers and made discoveries that revolutionized the field. Yet as their accomplishments grew in scale, so too did the gap between the credit they each received. While Joshua was awarded multiple prizes, Esther's name faded into the background, her gender proving to be a hindrance time and again.

Born in 1922 in the Bronx, Esther developed a self-determined personality early on. Her father was a Jewish immigrant from the Austro-Hungarian empire, her mother a first-generation American born to parents from Romania and Galatia. The family was poor, with Esther and her brother's lunches often consisting of a slice of bread with tomato juice squeezed on top; yet she dedicated herself to her studies and graduated from high school early at fifteen. She was a skilled linguist and received a scholarship to Hunter College, where for two years she enrolled in literature and French courses. As a junior, though, she radically shifted her major to biochemistry—much to her teachers' dismay. As a woman at the time, they said she'd easily find a job as a teacher in linguistics, but they warned that in science, her road ahead would likely be unpaved. Esther followed her gut, though, and, while completing her degree, she helped research the mold *Neurospora* at the New York Botanical Garden. Upon graduation, at only nineteen years old, Esther was accepted into a master's program in genetics at Stanford University, where the scientists George Beadle and Edward Tatum were researching mutations of the same mold.

Life at Stanford wasn't easy. In exchange for a room in a home, Esther did the household's laundry. George became her adviser, and she paid tuition by working as a teaching assistant for Edward; yet, to make ends meet, she and another TA would occasionally resort to eating frogs' legs after classroom dissections. But in 1946, with a thesis focused on one specific mutant strain of *Neurospora*, she received her master's degree—and, later that same year, she married another, younger scientist: Joshua Lederberg.

Together, the Lederbergs went to the University of Wisconsin, where Joshua had his first professorship and Esther earned her doctorate and then became a research associate. It was here that the two of them developed their individual professional careers as well as began their fruitful collaboration in jointly studying bacterial genetics.

The decade of the 1950s was an exciting time in the field. The period saw the discovery of DNA as the basis of hereditation and rapid advances in understanding the transmission of genetic material. In 1951, Esther herself discovered a strain of *E. coli* that contained a virus, which she named lambda phage. The lambda phage discovery had an immense impact on molecular genetics and virology: it was the first virus observed to live for some time inside a cell rather than killing it immediately after reproducing, which opened the doors for a better understanding of animal viruses such as tumor and herpes viruses. What's more, Esther proved that, upon isolation, the virus could be transmitted to other bacterial cells through sexual conjugation and recombination (types of processes through which bacteria or other low-level life forms mate or transfer genetic material to one another). This discovery soon led to the Lederbergs' joint discovery of "transduction," or the transfer of bacterial genes from one organism to another via phage.



A few years later, the Lederbergs made yet another discovery that revolutionized the study of genetics as the world knew it: replica plating. For decades, scientists had moved bacteria from one petri dish to another through a slow, labor-intensive process using a toothpick-like tool. One day, Esther wondered whether, instead of moving the bacteria clump-by-clump, she could rather pick up and move entire colonies. On a whim, she took out her compact makeup case and used the powder puff to give it a try. The initial experiment was successful enough that she and Joshua worked on refining the technique, using a specific sterilized Italian velveteen fabric that mimicked the material of her original puff. Their discovery of this technique in 1952 was, for microbiologists, akin to the invention of the printing press: they could conduct experiments with bacteria on what was previously an unimaginable scale in an equally unimaginably quick timeframe. The method was so effective that it is still used in labs today.

Using replica plating, the pair isolated bacterial mutations that they observed, discovered the origins of the mutations, and identified the mutations's key adaptive advantages. Namely, they demonstrated that mutations occur spontaneously in bacteria and do not result from environmental factors. Around the same time, Esther also recognized the bacterial fertility factor (factor F) and its role in DNA replication—a discovery that has proven to be essential in our understanding of how bacteria transfer genetic material.

Despite these major breakthroughs, the only prize the Lederbergs jointly received was the Pasteur Award of the Illinois Society for Microbiology in 1956. When Joshua received the Eli Lilly award in 1953, he affirmed that the prize should've been shared with his wife; however, as time passed, Esther's name became increasingly absent in the discussions and recognition surrounding their work, including in statements made by Joshua himself. Many of the papers they coauthored were published solely under his name, and in the few where Esther's name appeared, it was always secondary to his. Collaborating with Joshua had its advantages in the sense that his name opened doors and gave Esther access to labs where no other women were working at the time, but the benefits ended there.

The stark discrimination against Esther due to her gender revealed itself most prominently at that fateful Nobel Prize gala in 1958. Not only was Joshua receiving the Nobel Prize for research in which she had played a key role, but so too were her former mentors, George Beadle and Edward Tatum, for a discovery that she also had played a role in while working as their research assistant. While the three men received their awards, Esther sat quietly, listening to acceptance speeches that didn't even mention her name.

This could be said to have been the beginning of the end. In 1959, the Lederbergs returned to Stanford University Medical School. Her husband—three years her junior—founded and headed the Department of Genetics, while she was given an untenured position as a research geneticist. Then, following their divorce in 1966, Joshua went on to become the president of Rockefeller University, a biomedical research institution in New York, and was even honored with the United States' highest civilian award: a Presidential Medal of Freedom. Meanwhile, Esther was forced out of Stanford's genetics department and had to petition the dean for what ended up being a position at the same level she'd already had for fourteen years. It wasn't until 1974 that she finally became an adjunct professor—but even then it was still untenured, and effectively a drop in rank. In 1976, she gave up research to establish and direct the Plasmid Reference Center at Stanford, where she stayed until her retirement in 1985.

Shortly after her official retirement, Esther met Matthew Simon, whom she married in 1993. Matthew was Esther's biggest supporter in her later life, and today many of the intricate details about Esther are known thanks to him. Following Esther's death in 2006, Matthew spent over twelve years cataloging her photographs, papers, discoveries, and hobbies on the Esther M. Zimmer Lederberg Memorial Website, underlining her legacies that otherwise would have been forgotten.

It Runs in the Family

*Female scientists are to thank for some of the most essential understandings of human DNA*



One of the most famous photographs in the history of science is known as Photo 51. Taken in 1952, the image is a black-and-white X-ray–based fiber diffraction of a paracrystalline gel composed of deoxyribonucleic acid—in more relatable terms, it is a photographic representation of human DNA. And the vast significance of this photograph is almost indescribable. Capturing the structure of DNA helped solve one of mankind's greatest mysteries: what is life on Earth made of?

DNA, a self-replicating material present in not only humans but nearly all living organisms, is the carrier of genetic information, and it is passed down via reproduction, whether in an animal, plant, or fungus. Scientists had known about DNA's existence for years, but its exact structure—and thus the ability to study it further—remained a mystery until Photo 51. This visual evidence provided a key to unlock major advances in the field of genetics, including a better understanding of hereditary diseases in humans, identifying and classifying different animal species, and the improvement of personalized medicine.

While history has recorded some of the most groundbreaking genetic discoveries as the work of men, the true story is actually one where women made invaluable contributions to the field of human genetics. Photo 51 was produced by Rosalind Franklin and her lab assistant Raymond Gosling, though the credit for the discovery was officially given to three of her male colleagues. And Rosalind's story was not an isolated incident in 20th-century genetics: Nettie Stevens first discovered how a human's sex is determined by identifying X and Y chromosomes in 1905, and Marthe Gautier discovered the trisomy 21 genetic mutation that causes Down syndrome in 1958.

# Nettie Stevens

***1861–1912***

WHAT DETERMINES THE SEX OF A PERSON? This question perplexed scientists—and humanity at large—for millennia, and theories about its answer were wide-ranging. For example, Aristotle claimed that a human's sex was determined by the father's body temperature during conception, counseling "elderly men to conceive in the summer if they wished to have male heirs." Or, in 19th-century Europe, the nutrition of the mother's diet while pregnant was believed to determine the sex of the baby: poor nutrition would lead to male children, good nutrition females.

But in 1905, these far-fetched beliefs came to a halt with a revolutionary discovery: that of what would eventually become known as the X and Y chromosomes.

The question of sex determination fascinated geneticist Nettie Stevens. And in the early 20th century, the chromosomal theory of inheritance—in other words, what we know today to be fact, that the chromosomes you inherit from your mother and father determine what sex your offspring will be—was not yet accepted. Instead, it was commonly believed that gender was determined by the mother's health, or other environmental factors.

In her investigations, Nettie spent countless hours studying the sex organs of butterflies and mealworms under a microscope. While looking at the cells of the mealworms, she observed that females repeatedly had twenty equally sized chromosomes, while one of the male's twenty chromosomes was consistently and considerably smaller than the other nineteen. Nettie's findings were submitted to, and then published by, the Carnegie Institute in a book titled *Studies on Spermatogenesis* in 1905.

Nettie, however, wasn't the only geneticist hoping to solve this ancient mystery. Later that same year, her mentor, geneticist Edmund Wilson, published similar findings. However, his findings had one key difference: in his study, he had used an organism wherein the male has one less chromosome than females, which represented a completely different model of heredity, one that is not relevant to humans.

At the time she published her findings, Nettie was a novice. She had always been a bright student but was not afforded the luxury of wealth. In 1880, when Nettie was nineteen years old, it was not common for women to receive an education. Nonetheless, she graduated at the top of her class at Westford Academy in Vermont (from where, it should also be noted, she and her sister were two of only three women to graduate in an eleven-year period). After completing her initial studies, she was inclined to immediately attend college, but she first had to save money. Thus, Nettie began a career as a teacher, and sixteen years later, at the age of thirty-five, she could finally afford to enroll at the recently established Stanford University in California. Here, she earned her bachelor's and master's degrees before returning to the East Coast, where she completed her PhD at Bryn Mawr in 1903, at age forty-one—mere months before she began research for what would become her most important discovery.



Meanwhile, in 1905, Edmund was an accomplished biologist who had already been recognized for multiple contributions to the field of genetics. He was, in fact, one of Nettie's mentors at Bryn Mawr, and had also read her manuscript of her mealworm findings when it was submitted to the Carnegie Institute. Her book "is in every way a most admirable piece of work which is worthy of publication by any learned society," he wrote when asked for his opinion, "and I do not hesitate to recommend it to you for publication by the Institution."

Yet, due to his stature within the scientific community, when both his and Nettie's discoveries were published, his research overshadowed and gained more attention than hers. In the resulting historic canon, many textbooks now give Edmund full credit and erroneously cite Nettie as a mere assistant, if she is mentioned at all.

What's more, in 1906, one year after both Nettie and Edmund's papers were published, Edmund, along with Thomas Hunt Morgan (another of Nettie's academic mentors, despite being five years her junior), were invited to speak at a conference to present their theories on sex determination. Because the subject matter was so new, and the nature of these findings was so novel, this was likely one of the first times, possibly *the* first time, that a conference was being held where chromosomal sex determination was being presented as a theory to be taken seriously. Not only was Nettie not invited to speak at the conference, although she had published the vital paper theorizing chromosomal sex determination, she wasn't invited to the conference at all.

Their lectures speak to the fact that the significance of Nettie's and Edmund's discoveries was only accepted within the scientific community much later—so much later that Nettie's work was not fully recognized before her death in 1912, seven years after the publication of her book. Following her death, it eventually became clear that Nettie's conclusions were stronger and more accurate than Edmund's. Her findings became the standard for human sex determination, for the X/Y chromosome model. She had even noted that unfertilized eggs did not have chromosomal differences and that it was the smaller chromosome—later named the Y chromosome—carried by sperm cells that was responsible for sex determination. Edmund's conclusions, meanwhile, became the basis of the X/O heredity model, which is far less common in nature.

While Thomas Morgan eulogized Nettie upon her death, and her passing was notable enough to warrant an obituary in the *New York Times*, both she and Edmund are, more often than not, overshadowed by Thomas himself. Considered "the most important American geneticist in the first half of the twentieth century," Thomas was awarded the Nobel Prize in Physiology or Medicine for elucidating the role that chromosomes play in heredity in 1933—almost three decades after its initial discovery. It may have been Thomas who supplied enough evidence for the scientific community to finally accept Nettie's hypothesis (even though he himself refused to accept the chromosome theory until several years after Nettie and Edmund's papers were published) but it was Nettie—and to some extent, Edmund—who made the discovery.

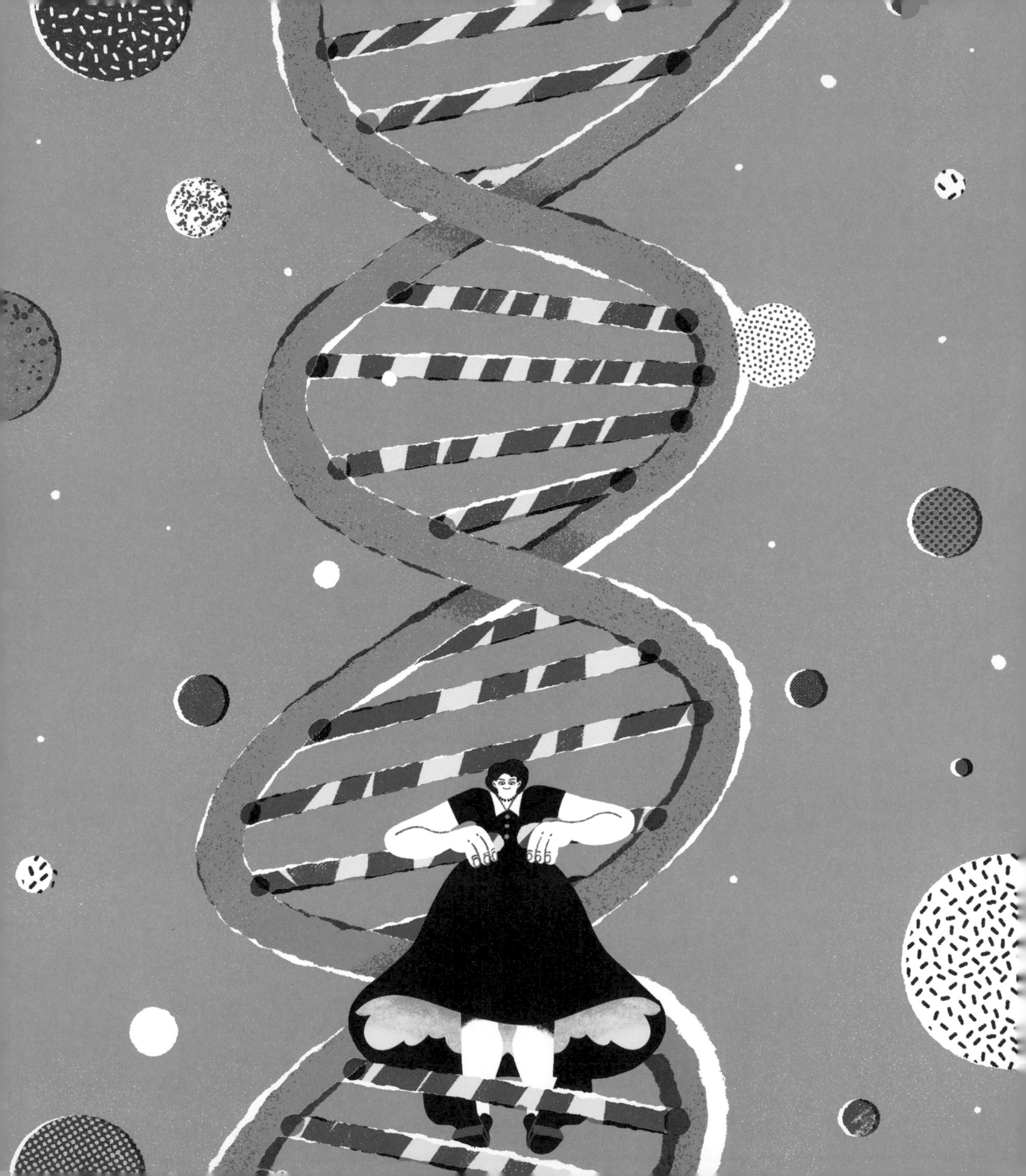

# Rosalind Franklin

***1920–1958***

AS A CHILD AND ADULT, ROSALIND FRANKLIN was never shy, never afraid to speak her mind, and never dissuaded from pursuing her scientific dreams—despite what society, and her family, told her to do.

Rosalind was born in 1920 in London to a prominent Anglo-Jewish family. Unlike the women of her time, and the women who came before her, who were only able to receive an education because of the uncommon support of their parents, Rosalind's father disapproved of women attending college. But, as her mother recalled, Rosalind set herself apart from her older brother, two younger brothers, and younger sister through her observations, perceptive judgments, and determined views; by age sixteen, she had defied her father's wishes and dedicated herself to science.

Not only that, she also chose to focus on physics, mathematics, and chemistry instead of botany or biology, which were more common among women in early 20th-century England. Following her studies at Newnham Women's College at Cambridge University, she worked for the British Coal Utilization Research Association. Her work on the porosity of coal soon became the subject of her doctoral studies, and she received a PhD in physical chemistry from Cambridge in 1945.

With her new title, Dr. Franklin moved to Paris to work in a laboratory, where she learned X-ray diffraction techniques—or, in other words, the ability to determine crystals' molecular structures. While living in a small room on the top floor of a house on rue Garancière, she refined her skills and became one of the world's finest X-ray crystallographers. After four years in Paris, however, she decided to return to London, where she had been offered a research position at the prestigious King's College.



Rosalind's successes early on in her career may sound like they came to her easily, but her determined mindset and persistence helped her find success in a field dominated by men. These same attributes, however, were also known to cause rifts among colleagues. The most prominent example of this happened at King's College, where there was an immediate misunderstanding and friction between Rosalind and her new colleague Maurice Wilkins. The scientists were both researching the structure of DNA, and were supposed to have done so together, but their divide deepened and they soon worked in relative isolation. Rosalind's arrival at King's

College in 1951 marked what has been called "one of the greatest personal quarrels in the history of science."

Maurice made small gestures to try to win Rosalind over and repeatedly offered his hand in collaboration, but his efforts were to no avail. Rosalind, confident in her abilities and jaded from having to prove herself in the workplace—an experience far too familiar for women in the 20th century—perhaps developed an unfriendly co-working approach. Nevertheless, finding himself alone in his own workplace, Maurice sought professional company at the Cavendish lab at Cambridge University, while Rosalind toiled on her own in London. At Cavendish, Maurice's friend Francis Crick was working with his colleague James Watson on building a model of DNA, parallel to Rosalind's research of the same nature. The race to determine the structure of DNA was on.

But as all researchers kept coming closer and closer to discovering the true nature of DNA, they all kept hitting their own roadblocks—that is, until Maurice secretly showed Francis and James some of Rosalind's work.

The work in question has become renowned as Photo 51, a stunningly clear X-ray photograph of a strand of DNA. The day Rosalind took the X-ray photograph and developed Photo 51 was the first time in history a human observed, with their own eyes, what this essential building block to all life on Earth looks like. Rosalind knew the gravity of what she had just achieved, and did not immediately share her discovery.

So, now equipped with Rosalind's Photo 51, James Watson and Francis Crick quickly succeeded in building a replica of DNA's now-iconic double helix structure, and in April 1953 their findings were published in a series of articles in the journal *Nature*. Although Rosalind contributed an article to the same journal providing further details on DNA's structure, the primary discovery was written about without a single mention of Rosalind's photo, even though it was imperative to—indeed, it was the foundation of—her male colleagues' revelation.

With the race to determine the structure of DNA finished, Rosalind soon pivoted to researching the tobacco mosaic virus. Using her X-ray crystallography skills, she discovered the virus's RNA structure, which then served as a model that helped other microbiologists break the human genetic code. At one point, she even corrected James Watson's interpretation of the virus's helical structure. She then took another turn and began investigating the virus that causes polio. But time wasn't on her side: in 1956, Rosalind was diagnosed with ovarian cancer, and she died only two years later at the age of thirty-seven. When her colleagues Aaron Klug and John Finch deduced the poliovirus structure in 1959, they dedicated their paper to her memory.

While Aaron and John acknowledged Rosalind not only in their paper but also when Aaron won the Nobel Prize in Chemistry in 1982 for his work on the structure of viruses, the same cannot be said of James, Francis, or Maurice. In 1962, the three scientists were awarded the Nobel Prize in Physiology or Medicine for their discovery of DNA's double helix structure. Rosalind couldn't have won the Nobel herself (they are never awarded posthumously), but she wasn't even mentioned in the men's acceptance speeches or in the surrounding media attention.

Her name only came to light in relation to the discovery in 1968, when James published his book *The Double Helix*. In it, he admits that the instant he saw Rosalind's Photo 51, his "mouth fell open and [his] heart began to race." And yet, he never once concedes that without Rosalind's work, he and James would not have had enough information to publish their groundbreaking paper. Beyond that, James's book cast Rosalind's character in a negative light—she was primarily made out to be a stubborn, data-hoarding scientist.

Today, asking whether or not Rosalind would have been included in the Nobel had she lived could be compared to asking if John F. Kennedy would have lived had he not gone to Dallas: the question can never be answered, but it can be said with certainty that Rosalind died unrecognized for crucial work that had, quite literally, been stolen from her lab.

# Marthe Gautier

*1925–2022*

IN 2014, MARTHE GAUTIER WAS PREPARING to give a speech, recounting her experiences as a female scientist. The speech was to accompany an award for her role in discovering the cause of Down syndrome. But the talk and award ceremony were suddenly canceled, mere hours before they were set to take place. She received the medal the next day in a small private ceremony. Marthe was eighty-eight years old. She made this discovery at the age of thirty-three. The talk was canceled due to a legal threat from the Jérôme Lejeune Foundation, which said it had reason to believe Marthe would "tarnish" the organization's founder, who had died twenty years earlier, in 1994.

Marthe, of course, had no intention of speaking illy of Jérôme. Rather, she simply wanted to accept credit that was long overdue and to speak openly about her experience as a young scientist in a sexist field in Paris. Marthe was born in rural France in 1925, the fifth of seven children. She was a keen student and initially developed an interest in Latin, but, in 1942, followed a path paved by her sister Paulette to study medicine in Paris. Paulette warned her sister: "If you're a woman and you're not the boss's daughter, you have to be twice as good to succeed." Marthe heeded this advice, especially after Paulette was killed by the Germans in World War II. As she wrote herself, she "aimed at the competitions that opened doors." Following the completion of her first degree and a medical clerkship, she was accepted into a prestigious internship program at Paris hospitals; she was one of two women among the eighty interns.

The first major milestone of Marthe's career as a pediatric cardiologist occurred in 1955, when she was awarded a one-year fellowship at Harvard University. She boarded a ship and set sail to the United States. After five days at sea, she had twenty-four hours to find an apartment and buy a bed, chair, and table before her position would begin. The fellowship was primarily to further her studies in pediatric cardiology, but in what later seemed like a lucky stroke of fate, she was also given a second job working as a lab technician. In this role, she advanced her skills in cultivating cell cultures and learned how to examine and photograph them under a microscope, as well as how to develop the resulting photographs.

Taking these skills back to Paris, she found a position at the Trousseau Hospital working in the pediatric unit led by Raymond

Turpin. It was a poorly paid part-time post, but Marthe accepted it with the long run in mind: as a woman, she'd need this job if she ever wanted to become an assistant—let alone an established—pediatrician. Raymond was interested in malformations of chromosomes, and in 1937 he had even hypothesized that Down syndrome (then called "mongolism") could be due to a chromosome abnormality. But his idea was only exactly that: a hypothesis with no conclusive evidence.

At the time, human cytogenetics—the branch of genetics that studies the structure of DNA within cell nuclei—was not yet well developed. It was only in 1956, the same year Marthe started working at Trousseau, that scientists came to learn that humans had forty-six chromosomes, not forty-eight, as was previously believed. The scientist who made this announcement to Marthe and her colleagues expressed disappointment that no labs in France were producing cells to study Down syndrome. Armed with her American experience of cultivating and examining cell cultures, Marthe stepped forward and said she was up to the task, if given the necessary space.



She was given a disused laboratory equipped with nothing more than a refrigerator, a centrifuge, and an empty cupboard with a low-definition microscope—better than nothing, she thought. Having received no funding, she then took out a loan to pay for the additional necessary equipment, including glass items and a distilled-water apparatus. Additionally, the products needed for cell cultures were not yet marketed in France. Not giving up hope, though, Marthe procured the products herself: she prepared fresh embryo extract every week; for plasma, she took blood from a cockerel that she purchased and raised in a garden; and for human serum, she extracted her own.

By late 1957, her lab setup was established, and she obtained tissue from healthy children to study. The controls, as expected, had forty-six chromosomes. Six months later, in 1958, Raymond provided her with tissue from children with Down syndrome. Marthe prepared the cells and placed them under the microscope, where she immediately saw an unmistakable difference: they had forty-seven chromosomes.

This additional chromosome, however, was small, and the microscope in her laboratory was not powerful enough to photograph its existence. In the preceding months, Raymond's protégé Jérôme Lejeune had begun paying regular visits to Marthe's lab, interested in her research. So, when her microscope proved incapable and Jérôme offered to take her slides and photograph them, she naively accepted.

Months of silence ensued, followed by a storm of unpleasant surprises. The first was when Marthe found out that the photographs—yet unseen by her—had in fact been shown at a conference in Montreal a few months after the slides were taken from her. Jérôme had presented them to the International Conference of Human Genetics and announced that he, alone, had discovered the cause of Down syndrome. The second shock came when Marthe learned that the discovery was to be published in the journal of the French Academy of Sciences: the paper was shown to her less than forty-eight hours before its publication. Jérôme was listed as the first author and Raymond the last; her name was squished in the middle, with her surname misspelled as "Gauthier."

At this, Marthe was hurt and suspected a degree of manipulation—a gut reaction that proved correct, as Jérôme continued taking credit for the remainder of his life. He convinced both himself and the world that he was the sole discoverer of the extra chromosome. He received numerous accolades, including one from US President John F. Kennedy, without ever mentioning Marthe (or Raymond, for that matter; his descendants eventually filed a lawsuit against Jérôme).

While Marthe does not dispute the fact that Jérôme indeed identified the extra chromosome as a copy of chromosome 21, she maintains that she was the first person to notice the abnormal count. The Jérôme Lejeune Foundation, however, continues to insist that its founder made the discovery, and—perhaps worried that the truth of Marthe's pivotal role might finally be accepted by the world—they continue to wield their power to silence her story. In 2009, in a reflection on this experience, Marthe wrote: "I have no happy memories of that period, as I felt cheated in every respect."

Coding New
Realities

*From the world's first computer to the invention of the tech behind Wi-Fi, women have been behind the digital revolution every step of the way*



Technology is a field notoriously dominated by men—and it has been since the dawn of the technocentric era. While some women have managed to claw their way into the industry, its culture remains one of a boys' club. With that in mind, it may come as a surprise that women have actually been at the forefront of the technology industry from the very beginning. And, in some cases, they were more than just trailblazers; they were its founders.

Before the digital age, computers were human. Toward the end of the 19th century, male mathematicians, physicists, astronomers, chemists, military persons, and more needed human computers to do the mundane work; computers spent days, even weeks, poring over complicated math problems. Given the job's tedium, to be a computer was seen as being no more prestigious than a secretary, and so computers were one of the only professional positions available to women.

Then, as electronic computers emerged, it was the female computers who first grappled with the new machines. Instead of doing calculations by hand, women devised how to program, and later they developed languages to make that programming easier. At the time, nobody thought being a computer programmer was an important job, so the skillset and the machines themselves were, at the very beginning, built by women.

In fact, it was a woman, Ada Lovelace, who invented the very concept of computer programming, ideated the first machine that could do what computers do today, and wrote the first computer algorithm. And it was six women—Kay McNulty, Betty Jennings, Betty Snyder, Marlyn Wescoff, Frances Bilas, and Ruth Lichterman, collectively known as the ENIAC Six—who programmed the first electronic computing machine and realized its full potential. Women also built and programmed the first personal computers, coined the term "software engineer," and pioneered programming languages. It was even a woman, Hedy Lamarr, who invented the technology now used for secure Wi-Fi, allowing computers to connect to the internet and maintain privacy.

The development of the technocentric era is enmeshed with female genius, yet these women's contributions have been sidelined from history. It was not Bill Gates of Microsoft, or Steve Jobs and Steve Wozniak of Apple, who first digitized and automated the world, even though they are often shown as the faces of the feat. Here, the spotlight is shined on the women who paved their path.

# Ada Lovelace

***1815–1852***

COMPUTERS HAVE REVOLUTIONIZED THE functioning of modern life, and the time span in which they've developed seems just as revolutionary. In the 1940s, one of the world's first programmable computers was built: the Harvard IBM Mark I Automatic Calculator, better known as the Mark I, was the size of a room, weighed five tons, and could crank out mathematical calculations in about six seconds. Today, an ordinary laptop or personal computer completes the same tasks in under a millionth of a second. But the engineers behind the Mark I took their inspiration from elsewhere, specifically from the work of a British inventor, Charles Babbage, who is credited with conceptually designing the first computer more than a century earlier. His imagined machine would have been able to calculate a complex mathematical calculation in about three minutes. The fact is, however, that the idea for the computer was not the product of Charles's inventiveness alone: the first computer was also conceived by—and the first computer program was written by—a young woman named Augusta Ada Lovelace, née King.

Ada was born in 1815 in London to a high-society family. Her mother, Annabella Milbanke, was a mathematician, and her father was the infamous Romantic poet Lord Byron, who called his wife the "princess of parallelograms." Given Lord Byron's unpredictable temperament, however, their marriage was short-lived: Annabella took Ada away from her father at the age of two months. Ada was lucky to have been born wealthy and noble, and to lead a relatively idle life, for it allowed her to gain an education privately and nurture her intellect. When she was four, her mother hired private tutors to ensure her education, and instructed that her lessons have a strong focus on math. Annabella wanted Ada to be schooled in rational thought, and she also wanted to avoid triggering any unruly traits that she might have inherited from Lord Byron. And in this atmosphere, Ada thrived.

By her teens, Ada was outpacing her tutors. She turned to self-educating herself through books, and struck up correspondences with some of England's most illustrious 19th-century minds, coming of age alongside the Industrial Revolution. In this way, she became friends with the well-regarded scientist Mary Somerville, and the logician Augustus De Morgan sent her problems to solve by mail. Upon receiving her responses, he remarked that Ada's "aptitude for grasping the strong points and the real difficulties [would have made her] an original mathematical investigator, perhaps of first rate eminence"—if only she'd been a man.

Undeterred by such comments, Ada continued to pursue her interests privately while simultaneously maintaining the swinging social calendar expected of London's elite. And it was at one such socialite party in 1833, when she was seventeen, that her privileges and intellect converged. Surrounded by peers, Ada heard a man introducing an invention he called the "Difference Engine." He spoke of something that could make reliable calculations with the crank of a handle, of a machine composed of precisely milled cogs and wheels that could store thousands of numbers, a machine that could automatically do what humans had been doing by hand for centuries. Ada, hearing this, needed to know more.



Shortly thereafter, Annabella took Ada to meet this man, Charles Babbage, at his home, where he had a prototype of the Difference Engine. Though incomplete, it fascinated Ada. In it she saw endless possibilities, and she asked Charles to mentor her. He politely declined her request, but they struck up a correspondence.

During their exchanges, Ada remained determined to gain his mentorship. "I hope you are bearing me in mind," she wrote to him in 1840, seven years after they had met; "I mean my mathematical interests." So, when she read a paper in a Swiss scientific journal in 1842 about a new machine Charles was developing, she saw her opportunity to impress him: she translated the paper from French, a language she had also learned growing up, into English. Moreover, she added her own notes about—and her own interpretations of—the machine. She had so many thoughts, in fact, that her notes were nearly triple the length of the manuscript itself. The results were published in 1843, and today the piece of writing is referred to as Ada's *Notes*.

Charles called his new machine the Analytical Engine; while he was never able to develop a working model of the earlier Difference Engine, he envisaged the Analytical Engine as a better, more accurate machine that would do much more than simple math calculations. And it would be gigantic, with tens of thousands of cogwheels, cranks, and rods designed to be powered by steam. In her notes, Ada described with unparalleled clarity how the device would work—better than Charles himself could. She illuminated its foundations in the Jacquard loom, a textile-weaving apparatus that embroiders images using punch cards. Like the loom could automatically weave silks, she explained, the Analytical Engine would weave algebraic patterns. It was, she liked to say, a "poetical science."

Ada's groundbreaking notes indeed caught Charles's attention, and from then on their correspondence increased in frequency, so much so that they often exchanged multiple letters per day.

In her notes, Ada explained much more than just the technical workings of the Analytical Engine. She imagined the impact it would have by crunching more than just numbers. She understood that if the machine could understand numbers, it would have the transformative ability to understand anything that could be represented symbolically, including more conceptual forms of knowledge like logic or music. With this, she articulated for the first time in human history the functioning of a general-purpose computer.

Furthermore, building on the system of the Jacquard loom, she concretely described a way to program the Analytical Machine with punched cards to weave a long sequence of Bernoulli numbers (a concept widely used in math, best described as a sequence of rational numbers that occur in analysis), without any assistance from a "human hand or head." And she backed this idea up with mathematical proofs. This part of her translation and notes, now known as Note G, is regarded as the world's first computer program.

Although the Analytical Engine was never fully realized, it represents the dawn of the computer age. When the first modern computers were finally built over a century later, Charles was remembered as the computer's first inventor. Ada's contribution, however, was forgotten until 1953, when the British scientist Bertram Vivian Bowden happened upon her *Notes* and republished them as part of his book *Faster Than Thought: A Symposium on Digital Computer Machines*. It was Bertram who first recognized that the idea of "electronic brains" began with Ada's foresight, rather than Charles's engine.

Today, Ada's groundbreaking modes of thought and inquiry are celebrated around the world, but her forward-thinking genius was un- and under-recognized for more than a century. The credit for her genius was, for a significant period of time, given to Charles, and scholars even disputed the fact that Ada had written *Notes*, despite her initials on the paper clearly indicating her authorship.

Finally, though, in the 1970s, the US Department of Defense developed a software language that streamlined a number of different programming languages and named it "Ada." This program is now used to power underground trains, airplanes, satellites, and rockets. And since 2009, she has been honored annually on October 15th, now deemed Ada Lovelace Day—a day to recognize and celebrate women in technology.

The ENIAC Programmers

# Kathleen McNulty, Betty Jean Jennings, Elizabeth Snyder, Marlyn Wescoff, Frances Bilas, and Ruth Lichterman

*1946*



THE ELECTRONIC NUMERICAL INTEGRATOR and Computer (ENIAC) was an eighty-foot-long, twenty-seven-ton, U-shaped metal monster built of conduit, black steel, wire, and eighteen thousand vacuum tubes. It had three thousand switches on forty panels, broken into thirty sections, each with its own mathematical function and punch-card equipment to receive instructions and print results. Fully built in 1945, ENIAC was the world's first all-electronic, programmable, general-purpose computer.

Before ENIAC, hundreds of human computers calculated bullet and missile trajectories, firing tables, and other complex equations during World War II by hand. With only pen, paper, and a desktop calculator, the calculus for a single ballistic trajectory could take forty hours or more to solve; no one could keep up with the thousands of equations the military needed in a given day. As a result, governments around the world were funding projects to develop computing machines to automate trajectory calculations and code-break enemy communications. One such project was ENIAC, funded by the US military.

Top secret and housed at the University of Pennsylvania's Moore School of Electrical Engineering in Philadelphia, ENIAC was designed by physicist John Mauchly and engineer John Presper "Pres" Eckert Jr. in 1943. But programming the machine proved a tedious, complex process, and it was another two years before ENIAC was functional.

To program ENIAC, it had to be rewired, replugged, and essentially become a custom computer for each new calculation; the process took days. Once the entire machine was set up anew, though, ENIAC executed calculations a thousand times faster than any computer—human or machine—had ever been able to do before. Every machine prior to it had either been mechanical or had involved mechanical elements. ENIAC, with its vacuum-tube switches alight with electronic pulses and signals, was the first fully electronic computer able to execute any type of computing function, once a program was written to instruct it.



Up until this point, human computing was a job given to women, as it was seen as nothing more than secretarial work. As human computing evolved into patching cables and writing programs, the view on the position didn't change: it was still regarded as an operational task, a mindless job for operators. As such, the female human computers were soon given the task of programming new machines, including ENIAC.

By 1945, six human computers had been put in charge of running ENIAC: Kathleen "Kay" McNulty (later Mauchly), Betty Jean Jennings (Bartik), Elizabeth "Betty" Snyder (Holberton), Marlyn Wescoff (Meltzer), Frances Bilas (Spence), and Ruth Lichterman (Teitelbaum).

But when these women, now known as the ENIAC Six, were given the job, no one told them they'd actually have to devise *how* to program it. The male designers and engineers who built it had only provided diagrams of the machine; there was no instruction manual. There was also no screen or keyboard, no programming language, and no operating system. Kay, Betty, Betty Jean, Marlyn, Frances, and Ruth had to figure out the room-size machine on their own. First, how to navigate it. Then, how to break down calculus equations step by step. Next, how to input a program by physically hand-wiring plugboards on the machine, using switches, cables, and digit trays. And finally, after fixing any bugs and double-checking calculations by hand, they could run the program and await results. They taught themselves what to do.

About ten months later, the ENIAC Six had become masters of the hardware *and* software, and in turn had become some of the first computer programmers in history: ENIAC was finally operational; the women had successfully run the first functional programs on the machine.

On November 30, 1945, the first confidential report on the completed ENIAC was published, describing how it operated and how it was programmed. Titled "Description of the ENIAC and Comments on Electronic Digital Computing

Machines," there were four authors listed: John Mauchly, Pres Eckert Jr., John Brainerd, and Herman Goldstine. Yet not one of these men—not even John M. or Pres, who had built it and designed what it was capable of conceptually—knew how to program the machine. John B. was the director of the ENIAC project, but he was not familiar with any scientific or technical aspects of the machine. Neither was Herman, who, as military liaison, was involved with ENIAC only so far as securing funding and reporting between the team of academics and army officials. Meanwhile, the names of Kay, Betty, Betty Jean, Marlyn, Frances, and Ruth, who developed ENIAC's arithmetic operations and programming methods, were nowhere to be found.

Soon after the report was published, and as World War II came to an end, ENIAC no longer needed to be kept under wraps. So, on February 2, 1946, it was presented to the press by John M. and Pres, albeit to little fanfare.

Twelve days later, however, ENIAC was scheduled to be presented again, this time to military personnel and scientists who would gather at the University of Pennsylvania. In the interim period, Herman and his wife Adele invited Betty, aged twenty-eight, and Betty Jean, only twenty-one at the time, to dinner. They asked the Bettys to set up a ballistics calculation to execute live at the upcoming demonstration. The programmers weren't sure it was possible to do in only a few days, but they knew they had to try.

The ENIAC Six worked around the clock on the requested trajectory program. But, the night before the demonstration, the program had an unsolvable bug: the Bettys had perfectly programmed the trajectory of the artillery shell, but the mathematical model said it would never stop: according to the punch card that the machine output, the imaginary artillery shell would crash through the earth at the same velocity it had had while flying through the air.

The morning of the demonstration, on February 14, Betty Snyder saved the day: alleging that she dreamed the solution, she knew exactly which switch out of three thousand to reset, and knew exactly which position, out of ten possible settings, it should be in. She flipped the switch; they were ready to present.

The demonstration was a massive success. John M. and Pres hosted the presentation, while the Bettys and Kay input the program and passed around copies of the printed results as souvenirs. Photographs were taken with Betty, Betty Jean, Kay, and their male colleagues, but in the media frenzy that followed, the front pages of newspapers across the country featured photos of only the men. Moreover, journalists misunderstood the machine, describing its capacity for memory and calling it a "thinking machine." But ENIAC had no memory, nor could it think; the real brains behind the computer—the women who programmed it—were, again, nowhere to be found.

Later that night, the university hosted a dinner to celebrate the demonstration, and none of the ENIAC Six were invited. In her autobiography, Betty Jean wrote: "It felt like history had been made that day, and then it had run over us and left us in its tracks."

Beyond the immediate misattributions and description of the demonstration and ENIAC itself, Herman blatantly lied in his 1972 book *The Computer from Pascal to Von Neumann,* claiming that he and Adele had programmed the February 14 demonstration. The military also later used one of the publicity shots from the event for a recruitment ad, but the three women were cropped out of the picture. Moreover, in the military's own press release about ENIAC, they said the machine was operated by a "group of experts," and only mentioned John M., Pres, and Herman by name. The ENIAC Six were erased from their own narrative.



It was only in the 1980s, when an undergraduate at Harvard University, Kathy Kleiman, was researching newspaper coverage from the 1946 ENIAC demonstration, that Kay, Betty, Betty Jean, Marlyn, Frances, and Ruth were rediscovered. Kathy noticed women in some of the newspaper photos, but the captions only identified the men in the pictures, so she began asking questions. Dissatisfied by being told they were models, Kathy eventually dug Kay, Betty, Betty Jean, Marlyn, Frances, and Ruth's names out from their buried places in history—and, in 1996, she realized none of the women, five of whom were still alive, had been invited to the official two-day event celebrating ENIAC's fiftieth anniversary at the US Army's Aberdeen Proving Ground in Maryland. Perhaps unsurprisingly, the ENIAC Six weren't mentioned in any surrounding press, either. Kathy spent the subsequent decades interviewing Kay, Betty, Betty Jean, Marlyn, and Frances (Ruth had died in 1986) and recording their histories with the goal of setting the record straight. In 2022, she finally published their full stories in the book *Proving Ground: The Untold Story of the Six Women Who Programmed the World's First Modern Computer.*

For decades, history did not remember Kay, Betty, Betty Jean, Marlyn, Frances, or Ruth; but today the ENIAC Six have been brought to light. As the University of Pennsylvania Engineering website states, the six "women who helped get the ENIAC off the ground [were] literally erased. . . . As modern engineers, we now celebrate the contributions of Kathleen Mauchly Antonelli, Betty Jean Jennings Bartik, Betty Snyder Holberton, Marlyn Wescoff Meltzer, Frances Bilas Spence, and Ruth Lichterman Teitelbaum." Finally, in 1997, all six women were inducted into the Women in Technology International Hall of Fame.

# Hedy Lamarr

***1914–2000***

HEDY LAMARR WAS ONE OF THE WORLD'S first legendary stars. When she immigrated from Austria to California in the late 1930s, she crash-landed into the film industry: as soon as her first film, *Algiers,* was released in 1938, every woman wanted her jet-black hair and her famous skirt-suits, and every (straight) man wanted to date her. For decades, she was known as "the most beautiful woman in the world."

In 1940, at the same time Hedy's star was skyrocketing, a secure radio-communications technology was invented. Called "frequency-hopping spread spectrum" (FHSS), it was conceived as a wartime weapon to make submarine-launched torpedoes undetectable and untraceable. It was revolutionary for the time—and also for decades to come. FHSS is now the foundational technology used in secure Wi-Fi, Bluetooth, cellular phones, and the Global Positioning System (GPS).

So, what do a mid-20th century celebrity and radio technology have in common? The answer is that Hedy invented it. But when she tried to offer the use of FHSS to the US military during World War II, they dismissed it, and then later confiscated her patent and applied the technology to every ship in the Navy. Hedy, however, barely received credit for her invention, let alone compensation, for a technology now valued at thirty billion dollars.

Born Hedwig Kiesler in November 1914, in Vienna, Austria, Hedy was an only child raised among the cultured ranks of high society. She attended private school and showed inventive prowess from an early age—at the age of five, Hedy took apart an old music box and put it back together again. Vienna, capital of what was at the time the Austro-Hungarian Empire, was also the hub of the Art Nouveau movement, which fostered modernism and was shattering classical, more conservative conventions. She was immersed in a bohemian world where women had careers and lovers outside of marriage; Hedy herself even modeled for photographers, with and without clothes.

In January 1933, at eighteen, Hedy experienced her first bout of public attention with her role in the film *Ecstasy,* wherein she appeared naked and acted out cinema's first on-screen orgasm. Adolf Hitler banned the film in Germany, partially for its explicit content and partially because of the heavily Jewish cast, Hedy

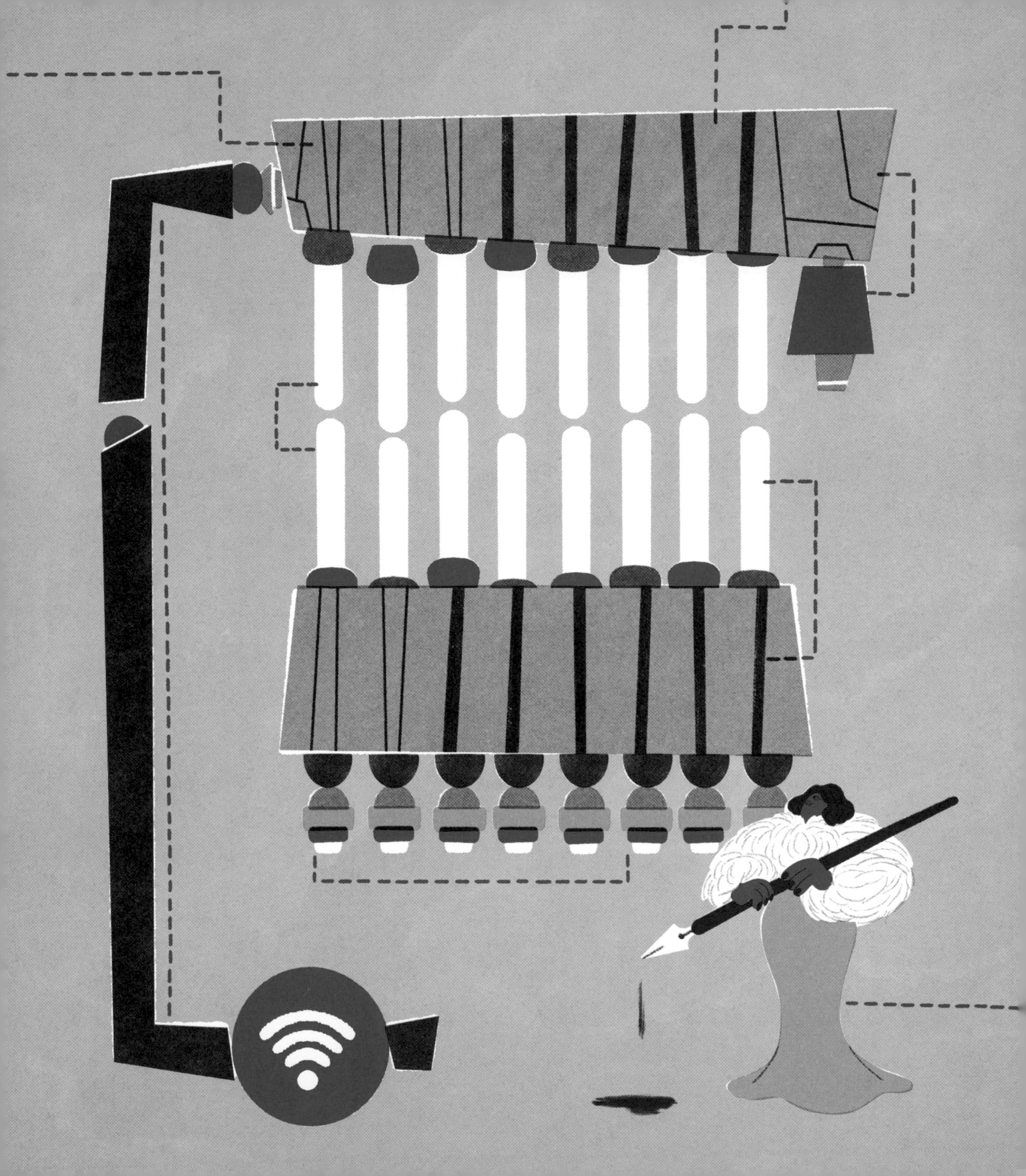

included; the Pope condemned it; and her father was livid. To rectify the blow to her reputation, she auditioned for and landed a lead role in a new, more modest theater production. By the time she was nineteen, she had married Austria's leading arms manufacturer.

As time went on, her husband became allied with the fascist governments of Germany and Italy. So when war became imminent, Hedy left her country and husband behind—forced to flee her marriage in secret, Hedy escaped on a bicycle, dressed as a maid. In 1937, she arrived in England, where she heard the American film producer Louis B. Mayer, of Metro-Goldwyn-Mayer, or MGM, was recruiting actors and actresses fleeing the Nazis, offering them contracts to come act in his films in Hollywood. Louis made Hedy an offer—$125 a week and a promise to keep her clothes on—but she declined and instead sneaked onto the same ship that was carrying Louis and his wife back to New York. Confined at sea, she wooed the producer, who made a second offer of about $500 a week (over $2,000 in 2022) and whose wife gave her a new name: by 1938, Hedwig Kiesler had become Hedy Lamarr.

Hedy journeyed from New York to MGM's headquarters in Los Angeles where, despite her growing fame and the grueling hours she worked, she never rested. She had a workspace set up in her house, as well as in her trailer on set at the films studio, where she explored her mind's inventions: a tablet that turned water into cola, a glow-in-the-dark dog collar, even a new shape for airplane wings for her then-boyfriend's aviation company. Finding the square format of airplane wings at the time inefficient, she incorporated features of the fastest birds and fish into a new, more aerodynamic design. Her boyfriend put her designs to use, and they soon became the standard for plane wings and remain so today. Yet Hedy never received any kind of official credit for this incredible idea.

By 1940, the world was at war, and the Axis Powers were winning. Hitler had taken control of parts of Western and Eastern Europe, was on the verge of invading Great Britain, and was waging a naval war in oceans around the world with German U-boats, or submarines. Torpedoes launched from the submarines were taking out Allied ships, and the outdated Allied equipment couldn't keep up. Hedy, wanting to help the war effort, put her mind to work.

Initially, she planned on quitting MGM and moving to Washington, DC, to join the National Inventors Council, a new governmental organization established to connect citizen inventors with the military and to promote citizens' development of viable ideas for the war effort. But before doing so, she had a flash of genius: a torpedo that hops between radio frequencies.

Hedy understood that militaries used radio signals to send messages and to guide torpedoes toward a target. She also knew these communications traveled on a radio frequency. So, if the enemy could detect the frequency being used, they could listen in on a message, jam it, or even hijack it, effectively intercepting and rerouting a message or a torpedo's pathway. Hedy concluded that if radio signals were transmitted along rapidly changing, or "hopping," frequencies, instead of on a single, stagnant frequency, radio-guided weapons and other communications would be undetectable.

With the invention conceptualized, Hedy recruited her friend George Antheil to help develop the technology that could solve the Allied Powers' problem. Using his experience building robotic orchestras and synchronizing player pianos (pianos that are automated to play a composition), George ideated a way to program both a torpedo and a ship to communicate codes across eighty-eight radio frequencies according to the same, albeit random, pattern. It was the ultimate encryption system.

In 1942, Hedy and George approached the National Inventors Council with their idea, who directed them to Sam S. Mackeown, a physicist and electronics expert. Sam then built the first working model of the frequency-hopping spread-spectrum device. Hedy and George received a patent for it that same year, and donated it to the Council; it was understood that, if the military used a donated invention, the patent-holders would be compensated accordingly. The Navy, however, ultimately seized the patent, citing it as the property of an enemy alien: Hedy was not yet an American citizen.

To add insult to injury, Hedy was told she'd be more valuable to the war effort using her fame to sell war bonds, instead of tinkering away at her inventions. She conceded, although she did not understand why the military considered her an illegal alien when it came to her invention, but when it came to raising money for the government, her alien status could be overlooked. She started making appearances anyways, putting on shows, dancing with troops, and selling kisses onstage. By the end of the war, she had sold around twenty-five million dollars' worth of war bonds (the equivalent of $343 million in 2022).

What's more, unbeknownst to Hedy, the military eventually did put her invention to use: in 1955, the Navy recruited another engineer to use the technology described in her seized patent to create a sonobuoy, or a floating device used to protect submarines, and later a surveillance drone. And by the early 1960s, all US naval ships were equipped with frequency-hopping radios.

After the war, Hedy spent millions of her own money self-producing and acting in three films. Alongside her fifth husband, she also bought land in what was, at the time, the small, indiscreet town of Aspen, Colorado, developing a ski resort modeled after her Austrian home. But her films, along with her other personal endeavors and marriage, ultimately failed.

She spent the remainder of her life largely living alone in New York City, and today, more than twenty years after her death, Hedy is most remembered for having had six failed marriages, for losing her fortune, and for her beauty. A ghostwritten "biography" published in 1966 focused almost exclusively on Hedy's tumultuous private life, and a secret communications expert even championed the falsehood that Hedy had stolen the frequency-hopping idea from her first husband, the fascist arms dealer.

But the true story of Hedy's life and her accomplishments as an inventor who created one of the technological foundations of modern society is finally coming to light. In 1997, Hedy was awarded the Electronic Frontier Foundation Pioneer Award and the Bulbie Gnass Spirit of Achievement Bronze Award. A biography that does her life justice, *Hedy's Folly,* was released in 2011. And the only retelling of Hedy's life in her own words—a buried 1990 interview with *Forbes*—was unearthed in 2015, laying the groundwork for the 2017 documentary *Bombshell: The Hedy Lamarr Story.*

# Who Runs the World? Women.

*From the university to the franchise business model, women built some of the world's most important structures*



Business, education, and government are three infrastructures that define the fundamental workings of our modern world. And the reality is that they have historically been the domains of men—and largely remain so.

First, there's business. There have been large strides regarding female entrepreneurship and, more generally, women's inclusion in the workforce over the last few decades (between 1970 and 2020, women have risen from comprising 40 percent of the workforce to 50), but according to the U.S. Department of Labor, the primary occupations women hold have barely changed. From the moment women entered the workforce in a meaningful way after World War II up until today, they have largely remained nurses, secretaries, (non-collegiate) teachers, cashiers, and other types of assistants.

However, women had a hand in developing corporate modernity. While history likes to credit Ray Kroc and the McDonald's fast food empire as the first modern instance of franchising, it was Martha

Matilda Harper who first successfully implemented this business model—and she did so decades before him.

Next, there's higher education. Women were barred from academia as teachers and students until the turn of the 21st century. Oxford, founded in 1096, did not fully admit women until 1920; Cambridge, founded in 1209, barred women from earning degrees until 1948; Princeton only opened to women in 1970. Even today, when it comes to providing equal educational access for people regardless of gender, the topic is still up for debate in many countries.

However, in 859 CE—long before the foundation of the Università di Bologna, which is frequently cited as the world's first university—Fatima al-Fihri established al-Qarawiyyin in Morocco. It was a mosque, madrasa, and library, but more importantly, it was the first degree-granting, multi-subject school in the world.

Lastly, there's government. Politics have inarguably been the realm of men throughout history. In 2022, a record number of women served in the United States Congress, and there were more elected female heads of state around the world than ever before. But in this historic congressional session, women still made up just over a quarter of the entire elected body. And out of 195 countries, only 24 had a woman head of state.

But, over 1,000 years ago in China, Empress Wu Zetian—to this day, the only female, outright leader of China—ascended to power and invented the concept of the civil service along the way.

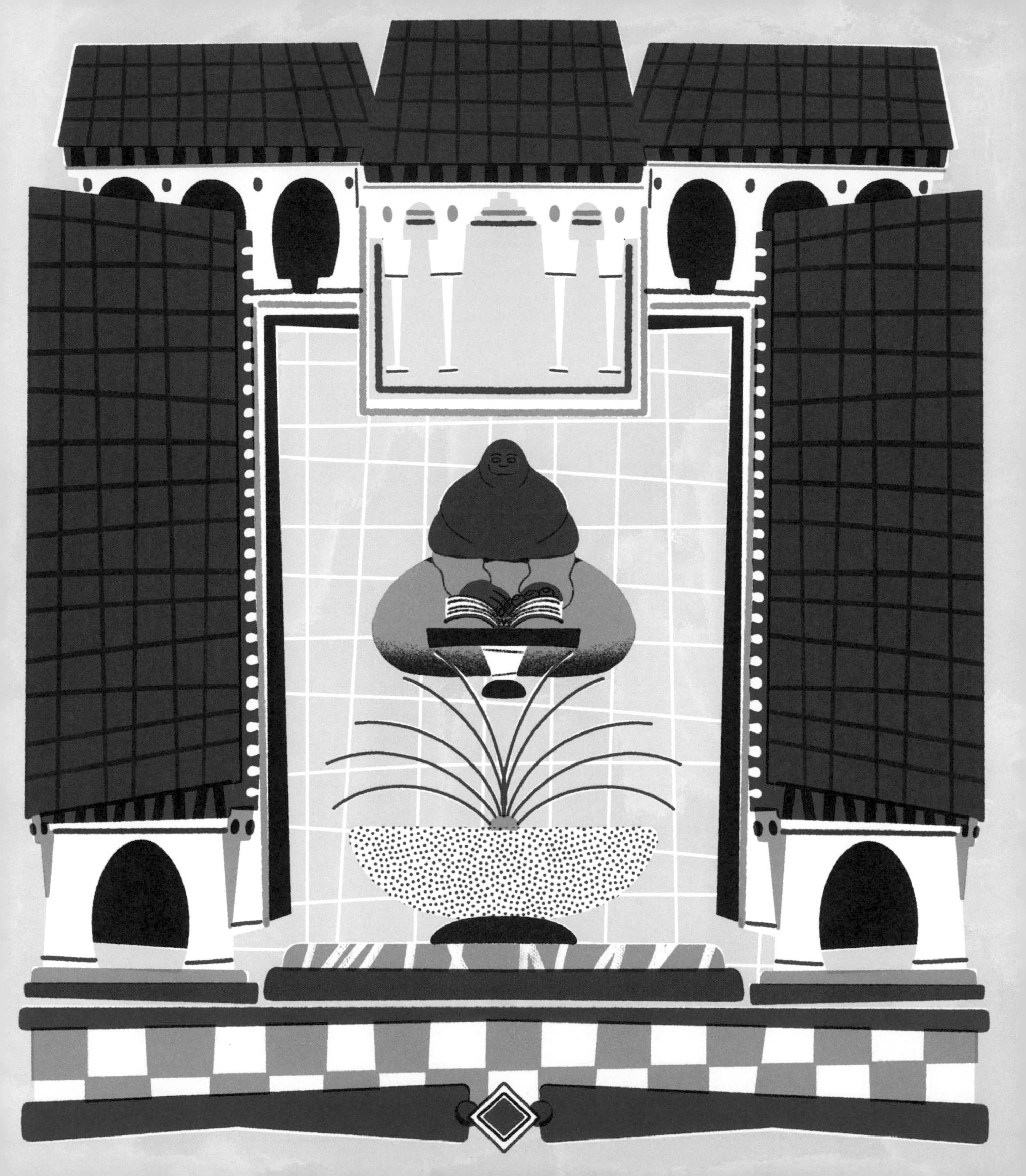

# Fatima al-Fihri

***800–880 AD***

MORE THAN A HUNDRED YEARS BEFORE THE word *universitas* came to be in Europe, the world's first "university" was already up and running in Fes, a city in modern-day Morocco. What's now known as the University of al-Qarawiyyin, founded by Fatima al-Fihri in 859 CE, was the first degree-granting institution of higher education in the world. Today, over a thousand years later, al-Qarawiyyin still stands as the oldest continuously operating university and library in human history.

Born in 800 AD, about a century following the death of the prophet Muhammad, Fatima lived during an early period of relative freedom for Muslim women. In pre-Islamic Arabia, society was patrilineal, and women were confined to domestic spaces. But Muhammad was explicit in giving women more personal rights: he allowed women to inherit property, to maintain their mahr (a type of dowry paid directly from husband to wife) after marriage, and even to ask for divorce. After Muhammad's passing, Islam burst out of the Arabian Peninsula, spreading through lands which are now Iran, India, North Africa, China, and Europe. In the midst of this tremendous expansion, Fes became a bustling metropolis.

Fatima and her family joined the mass migration of newly converted Muslims that was sweeping North Africa. Leaving Kairouan, in today's Tunisia, her family migrated westward to Fes. There Fatima's father became a wealthy merchant, but when he, her brother, and her husband unexpectedly died in rapid succession, only Fatima and her sister were left to inherit his vast fortune. With the money, they each decided to contribute to the community by funding the construction of new mosques.

When Fatima built her al-Qarawiyyin mosque in 859 CE, she also built a library and a madrasa—a school for Islamic instruction—and she didn't stop there. Fatima's madrasa (in 1965, the madrasa and library were officially renamed the University of al-Qarawiyyin) was the first of its kind in history: a school that offered degrees—and not only degrees in Islamic studies, but also in more liberal subjects like mathematics, astronomy, law, and poetry. It was a colossal structure for the time, and Fatima made sure that everything—from the magnificently detailed mosaic walls to the green clay-tiled roof—were built only with locally sourced materials. History also recalls that throughout al-Qarawiyyin's entire two-year construction, she fasted every day, from dawn until dusk.

Fatima died in 880 CE, shortly after the construction of al-Qarawiyyin, but her groundbreaking madrasa became the first and most important religious and academic center in the early Islamic empire. While Europe found itself in the darkness of the Middle Ages, scholars at al-Qarawiyyin were ascending into a Golden Age of science, medicine, and beyond. Alongside Islamic teachings, al-Qarawiyyin's halls were brimming with studies of Indian mathematical treatises, theories of Iranian statecraft, and the entire corpus of Greek written culture and literature. By the 1200s the al-Qarawiyyin Mosque was the largest in the world, and for centuries the madrasa and library hosted the most important Muslim, Christian, and Jewish scholars of the times.



With its proximity to Europe—separated only by the very narrow Strait of Gibraltar and 250 miles of land—the al-Qarawiyyin mosque, madrasa, and library helped channel enlightenment back into Europe, laying the groundwork for the European Renaissance as well as the foundation, in 1088, of the Università di Bologna in Italy, which has been inaccurately recognized for centuries as the world's first university. Moreover, the French mathematician Gerbert d'Aurillac, who became Pope Sylvester II in 999 CE, introduced Hindi-Arabic numerals (in other words, our modern numeric system—0, 1, 2, 3, etc.) to Europe only after studying at al-Qarawiyyin.

Perhaps even more significantly, it would have been unusual for women to attend al-Qarawiyyin, especially following Fatima's death. It wasn't until the 1940s—over eleven hundred years after its founding—that women were allowed to attend the University of al-Qarawiyyin in significant numbers. Furthermore, in Europe, it took more than eight hundred years for universities to allow women through their doors, and an added fifty for American universities.

Not only has Fatima's legacy gone unaccredited in the development of Europe's higher-education system, but universities and institutions of higher education were also, for so long, composed of male staff and student bodies. Yet the degree Fatima herself earned from al-Qarawiyyin, carved into a wooden board, still hangs in its halls today.

# Wu Zhao Zetian

**624–705 AD**

IN THOUSANDS OF YEARS OF CHINESE HIStory, only one woman has ever come to rule the land in her own right: Wu Zhao, later known as Empress Wu Zetian. But, after a lifetime spent shattering traditional Chinese gender roles, climbing her way from concubine to Empress outright, and promoting Buddhist ideology to challenge the Confucian status quo, when she died the slate was wiped clean, her achievements obscured, and her reputation forever tarnished.

Wu was born in what today is Shanxi Province, China. Her father was only a lumber merchant, but he descended from a family of high local standing and later became a high-ranking official under the rule of Li Yuan, also known as Emperor Gaozu, who founded the Tang Dynasty in 618. Given her family's standing, Wu received an education as a child and became well versed in music, history, and politics. She could also write poetry and traditional calligraphy. By the age of fourteen, her intelligence and beauty had caught the ruling Imperial court's eye, and she was appointed as a concubine to the second Tang ruler, Emperor Taizong, the son of Emperor Gaozu.

As a concubine in the fifth rank, she wasn't of great importance to the emperor, but receiving any rank at all was akin to winning a beauty contest at the time. She had proven both physical beauty and intellectual strength during the dawn of one of China's golden ages. China, at the time, was experiencing the opposite of Europe's Dark Ages: the country was undergoing significant political, economic, social, and intellectual development. Trade along the Silk Road was thriving, and the Tang Dynasty enjoyed far-reaching diplomatic and economic relations. The country hosted Persian princes, Jewish merchants, and Tibetan and Indian missionaries, and its developments surpassed that of both India and the Byzantine Empire. The center of the Tang empire was the most cosmopolitan of the world's cities.

Wu ardently observed what was happening around her and one day impressed Emperor Taizong himself with her radical spirit. The emperor was having difficulties training a horse, so he had turned to the court's women for advice. Wu replied, "I can control him [the horse], but I shall need three things: first, an iron whip; second, an iron mace; and third, a dagger. If the iron whip does not bring him to obedience I will use the iron mace to beat his head, and if that does not do it I will use the dagger and cut his throat."

It was a shocking response—and one that

foreshadowed some of the violence to come—but Emperor Taizong was pleased and gave Wu personal secretary-like responsibilities alongside her role as concubine. For the next ten years, she helped process official documents and learned useful skills necessary for conducting state affairs. She had risen from a low-ranked concubine to one of higher standing, thus having direct daily contact with the emperor himself.

Upon Emperor Taizong's death in 649, Wu was sent to a monastery, as was customary at the time: women who had served an emperor were sentenced to serving the rest of their lives in confinement, praying for their deceased lover's soul. But shortly thereafter, despite claims of incest, Taizong's son, the new Emperor Gaozong, invited Wu back to the Imperial court as his concubine in the second rank—the perfect place to pursue further ambition. She wanted to be Empress.

In the coming years, Wu bore four sons, followed by a daughter. One day, after Emperor Gaozong's wife, Empress Wang, played with the baby girl, she mysteriously died. Accounts of the time state that Wu killed her own daughter and blamed it on Empress Wang to turn the emperor against his wife. If that is what happened, the plan worked: Emperor Gaozong dismissed Empress Wang and promoted Wu Zhao to the position, where she assumed the name Empress Wu Zetian. Wu's first orders were the executions of Wang and Emperor Gaozong's concubine of the first order, as well as the exile of their relatives and supporters.

This was the beginning of Wu's rule. She soon controlled many affairs under the guise of assisting Gaozong, and in 656 she established her own secret police, who would remove any threat to her authority. Enemies and defectors were tortured and killed. Some political rivals were even forced to commit suicide. Then, when her husband suffered a severe stroke in 660, he assigned all state affairs to Wu, and when he died a few years later, her son ascended the throne. But the new emperor was just another puppet for her to control.



Wu virtually ruled the empire by proxy for ten years, and in 690, at the age of sixty-six, she finally took the throne. In ancient China, the sun was a fixed symbol representing the yang masculine, and the moon, the yin feminine; when Wu rose to power, she conferred upon herself a new name, one that spelled the sun and moon side by side. This was a shockingly transgressive act, not only because renaming yourself was a patriarchal privilege for fathers, but because by doing so Wu had all but eliminated her gender in a country that had deeply ingrained gender roles. Her rule could no longer be questioned because of her sex.

Ancient China was a civilization largely tied to Confucianism, an ideology that praised law and order. Historically, however, the gender ideals of Confucianism had a patriarchal outlook.

Women had few, if any, rights compared to men. In Wu's time, as China exported its Confucian ideas outside its borders, open trade routes also allowed new ideas to come in. The import that proved to be the biggest challenge to Confucianism was Buddhism; with Buddhism's many female deities and beliefs in reincarnation, traditional beliefs that men were more divinely privileged than women were rendered all but obsolete. Wu's embrace and promotion of Buddhism proved to be the key to securing her power, as well as the foundation for the Tang dynasty's inclusive and open culture regarding women.



For the next fifteen years, she pushed China into a new era. Empress Wu indeed used callous force and violence to reach this level, but such actions were not uncommon at the time; emperors throughout worldwide history did anything necessary to gain and maintain power, including committing cold-blooded murder. And despite the violence, what she went on to do for the country laid the foundations for several important social and economic developments.

The most significant change Wu made was to the process of recruiting Chinese officials. Previously, rulers chose their officials based on family ties and personal relations. Wu amended this process to place greater emphasis on candidates' educational levels and intellectual capabilities. No longer was the ruling class limited to a few powerful aristocratic clans. Instead, any talented and educated aristocrat, scholar, or military leader had a chance to be part of the Imperial court. This was the world's first example of professional civil service, as governmental positions were filled based on merit rather than family lineage or preferential treatment.

Wu also emphasized a bolstering of the Tang empire. Geographically, she conquered several regions and exercised cultural influence over Japan, Korea, and other parts of Central Asia. Economically, she focused on agricultural development, ordering the compilation of farming textbooks, the construction of proper irrigation systems, and the reduction of taxes. She even made the year 695 entirely tax-free. These policies greatly improved the life of common people and are still celebrated today with an annual agricultural festival.

Other areas of importance for Wu were the arts and women's rights. During her reign, she formed "Scholars of the Northern Gate," a group that promoted literary pursuits and helped create a culture of literature that flourished throughout the Tang Dynasty. She also organized a series of campaigns to elevate women's roles in society: she encouraged scholars to write biographies of significant women; she claimed that an exemplary ruler oversaw their country as a mother does her children; she also extended the official mourning period for a deceased mother to equal that of a deceased father—a groundbreaking and contested development for the time.

Empress Wu Zetian's policies continued to impact China's functioning for centuries to come. Upon her death in 705, however, her achievements were immediately pushed under the rug and her violent tendencies were instead put in the spotlight. Her daughter, niece, and prime minister—all women who held civil positions of power—were murdered, and historians immediately began recording Wu's rule as one of cruelty, black magic, and sexual impropriety. For centuries, she was remembered as an infamous, evil, and ambitious ruler.

Perhaps knowing this would be the case, she requested that her tombstone be left blank, expecting people of later periods to evaluate her achievements more fairly. She knew, after all, that she had changed the course of world history with her successful, novel government that stationed both men and women based on merit instead of favor. Yet today, thirteen centuries later, her tombstone remains uninscribed and her revolutionary rule is largely remembered as one of tyranny, that can be used as propaganda to discourage the rights of women to rule.

# Martha Matilda Harper

*1857–1950*

MUCH OF MODERN SOCIETY, AT LEAST IN the United States, is built on the franchise business model. Countless businesses, from restaurants to hotels to gyms, senior living facilities, and real estate agencies, are operated as franchises, and pretty much any commercial service-oriented venture that's a household name—Domino's, 7-Eleven, Ace Hardware, Crunch Fitness, Marriott—falls into the category. While the concept of the franchise is far from new (it was first recorded in the Early Middle Ages, around 470 CE), the franchise as it's known today didn't come about until the 20th century. And history likes to say it began with a man and a restaurant: Ray Kroc and McDonald's.

The truth is, however, that the modern commercial franchise business model was first experimented with in 1851 by Isaac Merritt Singer, founder of the Singer Sewing Machine Company, and the first successful small business to expand globally by way of franchising was not McDonald's, either. Rather, it was the now-little-known salon, Harper Hairdressing Parlor.

The Harper Hairdressing Parlor was founded by Martha Matilda Harper in Rochester, New York, in 1888. A few years earlier, she'd moved to Rochester from Canada at the age of twenty-five, where she worked as a servant, first for a local attorney and then for a wealthy woman named Luella J. Roberts.

Being at the service of others was nothing new to Martha: she'd been doing it since she was seven years old, when her father sent her to work for an upper-class farm owner in Ontario. Martha was the fourth of ten children, all of whom shared a one-room log cabin, and her family needed the money. In Ontario, she cleaned, cooked, and helped maintain the farm until she was transferred to the home of a nearby physician, who some historians believe was Dr. Weston Leroy Herriman and who sought household help in the wake of his wife's death. It just so happened that Weston had a particular interest in hair and its physiology.

At the turn of the 20th century, hair-care regimens were minimal. Men and women alike rarely washed their hair, and when they did, it was with crude soap made most frequently from hog fat and ashes. Weston, though, spent his time studying things like scalp hygiene and the effects of brushing one's hair. Martha was often at his side, observing and listening as he shared his knowledge.

When Weston died in 1879, he bequeathed to Martha something that soon became invaluable: a secret recipe for an all-natural hair tonic—in today's words, an organic shampoo. With not much more than the formula and a small amount of savings in a knotted handkerchief, Martha decided to cross the border and emigrate to Rochester.

When she started working for Luella, Martha assumed the role of her personal beautician—for when hair-care regimens were performed, they were done in private. Martha began applying Weston's methods, giving Luella scalp massages to stimulate hair growth and washing her hair with the tonic, which she named the Moscano Tonique and started producing in Luella's back yard. Luella, so impressed with Martha's skills and the results, raved to her friends and invited them to her house to receive treatments themselves.

Before long, Martha was delivering the tonic door to door and sensed a business opportunity. The odds were stacked against her—Rochester may have been home to the burgeoning women's suffrage movement led by Susan B. Anthony, but the entrepreneurial landscape remained male-dominated—yet she decided to go for it anyway.

With the help of a lawyer after her first rental application was denied, she secured a space in the city's most prestigious office building and invested her life savings of $360 (around $10,500 in 2022) to open the doors of Harper Hairdressing Parlor.



Despite her thriving at-home service and her years-long training in pampering others, though, the salon was far from an overnight success. Women balked at the idea of getting their hair done in public. But one day, she had an idea: the children's music school next door didn't have a waiting room, so she told the mothers they could wait in her salon. Soon enough, they weren't just idly waiting but having their hair washed, scalps massaged, and hair coiffed according to the day's fashions.

Martha's salon soon counted the city's most elite women as customers. She became known for the Moscano Tonique, which she patented, and the two-hour-long "Harper Method" treatment, which involved head and shoulder massages, facials, and procedures called the "saddle maneuver," "strapping action," and "checking motion" that supposedly stimulated blood flow and promoted hair growth. With her own floor-length chestnut hair, she was a walking advertisement for herself. (Her hair was so incredible that P. T. Barnum once even tried recruiting her for the circus.)

Customer service was at the center of the Harper Method. In an effort to improve her clients' experiences, she even invented the reclining shampoo chair and a wash basin with a semi-circle cut out for one's neck—the same type of chair that populates every hair salon today. Her clientele continued to grow, and prominent women from other cities started visiting too.

Before long, Martha was receiving requests to open salons in other cities, but she refused to open additional locations until a certain number of women in the city signed a petition. When a petition was signed by twenty-five people in a city, she would search for operators she could trust; she knew she had to maintain control over the Harper Method, including the level of service and products offered. She also sought to give the opportunity to run a business to women from similar backgrounds to her own—women who had the drive and discipline to do so but lacked the start-up capital. Once she found an operator, Martha asked the new "Harperite" to pay a fee (paid as a loan over time) and to agree to stock only Harper products, which now included tonics, chairs, and sinks as well as brushes. Knowing the various roles women juggle, she also allowed salon operators to take time off during the day when needed, and she offered clients complimentary childcare and evening hours at the salons.

Three years after her opening in Rochester, Martha's second location opened in 1891 in Buffalo, New York. Locations soon appeared in Detroit, Chicago, San Francisco, and Baltimore. By 1914, Martha had opened 134 franchises across the US, Canada, England, France, and Germany. Then, between 1920 and 1921 alone, the number of franchises jumped from 175 to 350. At this point, Martha also expanded her services to include offerings for men, and she sold her products in department stores.

By the time she died in 1950, at ninety-three years old, Martha's business had grown into an empire: she had five hundred salons around the world and had counted US President Woodrow Wilson, Susan B. Anthony, First Ladies Jacqueline Kennedy and Lady Bird Johnson, the British royal family, and members of the Vanderbilt, Ford, Hearst, and DuPont families as clients.

But Martha's success and notoriety ended with her life.

In 1920, Martha had married Robert MacBain, who was twenty-four years her junior. When she started experiencing signs of dementia and eventually died, he assumed control of the business. Under him, the quality meticulously upheld by Martha began to suffer. Robert introduced, for example, synthetic products like chemical dyes and perms into the salons' offerings—products that had been strictly forbidden by Martha. Plus, with a man in charge, the female *esprit de corps* that had laid the foundations of the company began to disappear.

A mere six years after Martha's death in 1950, the company had already become a shadow of what it once had been, and Robert sold it. From 1956 until 1972, it bounced among various hands, never regaining the prominence it once had enjoyed. And when an ex-Harper chemist who had opened their own salon bought it in 1972, they closed the training center's doors, and the salons slowly but surely disappeared. The last salon standing—which happened to be the original salon in Rochester—closed its doors in 2005.

Today, Martha Matilda Harper and the Harper Method hardly ring any bells, but they should—in the same way McDonald's and Ray Kroc go hand in hand. Martha successfully implemented the first service-oriented franchise in the world, over half a century before Ray. She also pioneered the idea of the hair salon on a global level and invented the chairs that every hairdresser still relies on. Yet it was only upon the publication of Jane Plitt's biography *Martha Matilda Harper and the American Dream* in 2000 that Martha's achievements started to gain recognition: in 2001 she was posthumously honored with an award from the International Franchising Association, in 2003 she was inducted into the National Women's Hall of Fame, and various articles have been published about her in the years since. But in the overarching history of the franchise business model, her name is almost entirely absent while Ray Kroc remains at the forefront.

# Resources/Bibliography


### Epigraph

Ocasio-Cortez, Alexandria (@AOC), "They'll tell you you're too loud—that you'll need to wait your turn; and ask the right people permission. Do it anyway." Twitter, March 9, 2018, 9:04 p.m., https://twitter.com/aoc/status/972292022362165249.

## Women Writing History

### Enheduanna

Forman, Amanda, Dr. "Civilisation." Episode 1. *The Ascent of Woman*. Directed by Hugo Macgregor. BBC Two, 2015.

Meador, Betty De Shong. *Inanna, Lady of Largest Heart: Poems of the Sumerian High Priestess*. University of Texas Press, 2001.

Meador, Betty De Shong. *Princess, Priestess, Poet: The Sumerian Temple Hymns of Enheduanna*. University of Texas Press, 2009.

### Murasaki Shikibu

Forman, Amanda, Dr. "Separation." Episode 2. *The Ascent of Woman*. Directed by Hugo Macgregor, BBC Two, 2015.

Shikibu, Murasaki. *The Tale of Genji*. Translated by Edward Seidensticker. Knopf, 1992.

### Mary Shelley

Scholes, Robert, and Eric S. Rabkin. *Science Fiction: History, Science, Vision*. Oxford University Press, 1977.

Shelly, Mary. *Frankenstein*. Penguin Classics, 2012.

### Judy Malloy

Coover, Robert. "The end of books." *New York Times*, June 21, 1992. https://timesmachine.nytimes.com/timesmachine/1992/06/21/153793.html.

Malloy, Judy. Artist Statement in *Uncle Roger*. UNIX and BASIC version, 1986–1988. Web version, 1995. https://collection.eliterature.org/3/works/uncle-roger/statement.html.

Malloy, Judy. "Digital Literature Pioneers: Judy Malloy on 'narrabases'." *News* (blog). *The Lit Platform*, April 24, 2014. https://theliteraryplatform.com/news/2014/04/digital-literature-pioneers-judy-malloy-on-narrabases-80s-silicon-valley-and-e-literature-today/.

## There's More to Art than Meets the Eye

### Hilma af Klint

Fant, Åke. *Hilma af Klint: Occult Painter and Abstract Pioneer*. Translated by Ruth Urbom. Bokförlaget Stolpe, 2021.

Ferren, Andrew. "In Search of Hilma af Klint, Who Upended Art History, But Left Few Traces." *New York Times*, October 21, 2019. https://www.nytimes.com/2019/10/21/travel/stockholm-hilma-af-klint.html.

"The Forgotten Genius of Hilma af Klint." *News* (blog). 52 *Insights*, April 10, 2016. https://www.52-insights.com/news/the-forgotten-genius-of-hilma-af-klint-art/.

Giuggenheim. "Hilma af Klint: Paintings for the Future." Past Exibitions. https://www.guggenheim.org/exhibition/hilma-af-klint.

Moderna Museet. "About the Artist Hilma af Klint." https://www.modernamuseet.se/stockholm/en/exhibitions/hilma-af-klint-2013/about-the-artist/.

Scott, A. O. "'Beyond the Visible: Hilma af Klint' Review: What Did She See, and When?" Review of *Beyond the Visible—Hilma af Klint*, directed by Halina Dyrschka. *New York Times*, April 16, 2020. https://www.nytimes.com/2020/04/16/movies/beyond-the-visible-hilma-af-klint-review.html.

Smith, Roberta. "'Hilma Who?' No More." *New York Times*, October 11, 2018. https://www.nytimes.com/2018/10/11/arts/design/hilma-af-klint-review-guggenheim.html.

### Alice Guy Blaché

Green, Pamela E., dir. *Be Natural: The Untold Story of Alice Guy-Blanché*. Be Natural Productions, 2018.

Simon, Joan, ed. *Alice Guy Blaché: Cinema Pioneer*. With contributions by Jane M. Gaines, Alison McMahan, Charles Musser, Kim Tomadjoglou, and Alan Williams. Yale University Press, 2009.

### Lillie P. Bliss, Abby Aldrich Rockefeller, and Mary Quinn Sullivan

Hudes, Karen. "The Life and Lasting Impact of Abby Aldrich Rockefeller." *The Center Magazine*, August 11, 2022. https://www.rockefellercenter.com/magazine/arts-culture/abby-aldrich-rockefeller-moma/.

Kramer, Hilton. "The Man Who Created MOMA." *The New Criterion*, December 2001. https://newcriterion.com/issues/2001/12/the-man-who-created-moma.

MoMA. "Modern Women: A Partial History." Modern Women: Women Artists at the Museum of Modern Art. https://www.moma.org/interactives/modern_women/history/.

MoMA. "The Museum of Modern Art History." About Us. https://www.moma.org/about/who-we-are/moma-history.

MoMA. "Three Women Have a Vision." MoMA through Time. https://www.moma.org/interactives/moma_through_time/1920/three-women-have-a-vision/.

Reynolds, Lindsey. "The Expeditionists: Pioneering Women Who Traveled the World on Collecting Expeditions." *Inside/Out: A MoMA/MoMA PS1 Blog*, June 13, 2012. https://www.moma.org/explore/inside_out/2012/06/13/the-expeditionists-pioneering-women-who-traveled-the-world-on-collecting-expeditions/.

Takac, Balasz. "The Revolutionary Career of MoMA Director Alfred H. Barr Jr." Widewalls. June 25, 2021. https://www.widewalls.ch/magazine/alfred-h-barr-jr-moma.

### Janet Sobel

Barcio, Phillip. "Shedding Light on the Drip Paintings by Janet Sobel." *IdeelArt* (Blog), January 28, 2019. https://www.ideelart.com/magazine/janet-sobel.

Blackstone, Maya. "Overlooked No More: Janet Sobel, Whose Art Influenced Jackson Pollock." *New York Times*, July 30, 2021. https://www.nytimes.com/2021/07/30/obituaries/janet-sobel-overlooked.html.

Braverman, Laura. "Janet Sobel: American, born Ukraine. 1894–1968." MoMA. https://www.moma.org/artists/5503.

Hill, Isabella. "Janet Sobel: Forgotten Female Artist Who Influenced Jackson Pollock." Women Artists, *Daily Art Magazine*, October 15, 2022. https://www.dailyartmagazine.com/janet-sobel-forgotten-female-artist/.

Zalman, Sandra. "Janet Sobel: Primitive Modern and the Origins of Abstract Expressionism." *Woman's Art Journal* 36, no. 2 (Fall/Winter 2015): 20–29. https://www.jstor.org/stable/26430653.

## Music to a Woman's Ears

### Maria Anna Mozart

Classic FM. "Was Mozart's Sister Actually the Most Talented Musician in the Family?" Mozart, April 8, 2021. https://www.classicfm.com/composers/mozart/nannerl-mozarts-sister-better-musician/.

Hall, Sophia Alexandra. "Mozart Claimed Credit for His Sister's Compositions, Says Former Conductor Turned Professor." Mozart, Classic FM, January 10, 2022. https://www.classicfm.com/composers/mozart/claimed-credit-sister-compositions/.

Leung, Jacqueline. "Nannerl Mozart: Neglected Sister or Wolfgang's Childhood Muse?" *Piano Performer Magizine* 2 (June 21, 2016). http://magazine.pianoperformers.org/nannerl_piano_performer_magazine_summer_issue_2016/.

Rusch, Elizabeth. "Maria Anna Mozart: The Family's First Prodigy." *Smithsonian Magazine*, March 27, 2011. https://www.smithsonianmag.com/arts-culture/

maria-anna-mozart-the-familys-first-prodigy-1259016/.

"A Visit to Mozart's Sister." *The Musical Times* 132, No. 1786, Mozart Supplement: Facsimile of the Musical Times Mozart Centenary Issue for December 1891 (Dec. 1991): 27–28. https://www.jstor.org/stable/966562.

**Fanny Mendelssohn**

Forbes, Malcolm, and Jeff Bloch. *Women Who Made a Difference.* Simon & Schuster, 1991.

Kimber, Marian Wilson. "The 'Suppression' of Fanny Mendelssohn: Rethinking Feminist Biography." *19th-Century Music* 26, no. 2 (2002): 113–129. https://doi.org/10.1525/ncm.2002.26.2.113.

Saffle, Michael. Review of *Fanny Mendelssohn Hensel: Her Contributions to Nineteenth-Century Musical Life*, by Carol Lynelle Quin. *Bulletin of the Council for Research in Music Education*, no. 80 (Fall 1984): 70–75. https://www.jstor.org/stable/40317872.

Todd, R. Larry. *Fanny Hensel: The Other Mendelssohn.* Oxford University Press, 2009.

Todd, R. Larry. "Secret Aspirations (1830–1833)." In *Fanny Hensel: The Other Mendelssohn*, 146–172. New York: Oxford University Press, 2009. https://oxford.universitypressscholarship.com/view/10.1093/acprof:oso/9780195180800.001.0001/acprof-9780195180800-chapter-6.

Werner, Eric. "New Light on the Family of Felix Mendelssohn." *Hebrew Union College Annual* 26 (1955): 543–565. http://www.jstor.org/stable/23506159.

**Rosetta Nubin, aka Sister Rosetta Tharpe**

Bailey, Brooke. *The Remarkable Lives of 100 Women Artists (20th Century Women).* Adams Media, 1994.

Molenda, Michael. *Guitar Player Presents 50 Unsung Heroes of the Guitar.* Backbeat Books, 2011.

O'Dair, Barbara. *The Rolling Stone Book of Women in Rock: Trouble Girls.* Random House, 1997.

Santelli, Robert. *American Roots Music (Based on the PBS Television Series).* Abrams, 2001.

Sawyers, June Skinners. *10 Songs that Changed the World.* Murdoch Books, 2009.

Wald, Gayle. *Shout, Sister, Shout!: The Untold Story of Rock-and-Roll Trailblazer Sister Rosetta Tharpe.* Beacon Press, 2007.

**Willie Mae Thornton, aka Big Mama Thornton**

Brunning, Bob. *Blues: The British Connection.* Brandford Press, 1986.

Lauterbach, Preston. *The Chitlin' Circuit and the Road to Rock 'N' Roll.* W. W. Norton, 2012.

Ochs, Meredith. *Rock and Roll Women: The 50 Fiercest Female Rockers.* Sterling Publishing Co., 2018.

Padgett, Ray. *Cover Me: The Stories Behind the Greatest Cover Songs of All Time.* Sterling Publishing Co., 2017.

Sawyers, June Skinners. *10 Songs that Changed the World.* Murdoch Books, 2009.


## Taking to the Streets


**Pauli Murray**

Yale University. "Anna Pauline (Pauli) Murray, Yale 1965 J.S.D., 1979 Hon. D.Div." Office of Public Affairs & Communications. https://communications.yale.edu/media/media-kits/anna-pauline-pauli-murray-yale-1965-jsd-1979-hon-ddiv.

Schulz, Kathryn. "The Many Lives of Pauli Murray." *New Yorker*, April 10, 2017. https://www.newyorker.com/magazine/2017/04/17/the-many-lives-of-pauli-murray.

Murray, Pauli. *Song in a Weary Throat: Memoir of an American Pilgrimage.* With a new introduction by Patricia Bell-Scott. New York: Liveright Publishing, 2018.

**Anna Arnold Hedgeman and Dorothy Height**

Fox, Margalit. "Dorothy Height, Largely Unsung Giant of the Civil Rights Era, Dies at 98." *New York Times*, April 20, 2010. https://www.nytimes.com/2010/04/21/us/21height.html.

Height, Dorothy. *Open Wide the Freedom Gates: A Memoir.* With a forward by Maya Angelou. PublicAffairs, 2005.

NAACP. "The 1963 March on Washington." https://naacp.org/find-resources/history-explained/1963-march-washington.

National Museum of American History. "Changing America: The Emancipation Proclamation, 1863, and the March on Washington, 1963." https://americanhistory.si.edu/changing-america-emancipation-proclamation-1863-and-march-washington-1963/1963/leaders-march.

Scanlon, Jennifer. *Until There Is Justice: The Life of Anna Arnold Hedgeman.* Oxford University Press, 2016.

Stewart, Jocelyn. "Dorothy Height Dies at 98; Civil Rights Leader Fought for Women's, Children's Issues." *Los Angeles Times*, April 21, 2010. https://www.latimes.com/archives/la-xpm-2010-apr-21-la-me-dorothy-height-20100421-story.html.


## Down to Earth


**Maria Sibylla Merian**

Klein, Joanna. "A Pioneering Woman of Science Re-Emerges after 300 Years." *New York Times*, January 23, 2017. https://www.nytimes.com/2017/01/23/science/maria-sibylla-merian-metamorphosis-insectorum-surinamensium.html.

Manning, Patrick, and Daniel Rood, eds. "The History and Influence of Maria Sibylla Merian's Bird-Eating Tarantula: Circulating Images and the Production of Natural Knowledge." In *Global Scientific Practice in the Age of Revolutions, 1750–1850*, 54–70. University of Pittsburgh Press, 2016.

Rowland, Ingrid D. "The Flowering Genius of Maria Sibylla Merian." *The New York Review*, April 9, 2009. https://www.nybooks.com/articles/2009/04/09/the-flowering-genius-of-maria-sibylla-merian/.

Valiant, Sharon. "Maria Sibylla Merian: Recovering an Eighteenth-Century Legend." *Eighteenth-Century Studies* 26, no. 3 (Spring1993),: 467–79. https://doi.org/10.2307/2739414.

Wulf, Andrea. "The Woman Who Made Science Beautiful." *The Atlantic*, January 19, 2016. https://www.theatlantic.com/science/archive/2016/01/the-woman-who-made-science-beautiful/424620/.

**Mary Anning**

Goodhue, Thomas W. *Curious Bones: Mary Anning and the Birth of Paleontology.* Morgan Reynolds, 2002.

Stille, Darlene. *Extraordinary Women Scientists*, 16–18. Children's Press, 1995.

**Marie Tharp**

Bressan, David. "July 30, 1920: Marie Tharp, the Woman Who Discovered the Backbone of Earth." *History of Geography* (blog). *Scientific American*, July 30, 2013. https://blogs.scientificamerican.com/history-of-geology/july-30-1920-marie-tharp-the-woman-who-discovered-the-backbone-of-earth/.

Columbia Climate School Lamont-Doherty Observatory. "About Marie Tharp." https://marietharp.ldeo.columbia.edu/about-marie-tharp.

Doel, Ronald E., Tanya J. Levin, and Mason K. Marker. "Extending Modern Cartography to the Ocean Depths: Military Patronage, Cold War Priorities, and the Heezen–Tharp Mapping Project, 1952–1959." *Journal of Historical Geography* 32, no.3 (July 2006): 605-626. https://doi.org/10.1016/j.jhg.2005.10.011.

Hall, Stephen S. "The Contrary Map Maker." *New York Times Magazine*, December 31, 2006. https://www.nytimes.com/2006/12/31/magazine/31Tharp.t.html.

Mason, Betsy. "How One Brilliant Woman Mapped the Ocean Floor's Secrets." *National Geographic*, February 15, 2017. https://www.nationalgeographic.com/culture/article/marie-tharp-map-ocean-floor.

**Gladys Mae West**

Dyson, Cathy. "Glady's West's Work on GPS 'Would Impact the World.'" *AP News*, February 3, 2018. https://apnews.com/article/2dee50a4b-3be4564b417f7f569b38ba4.

Madrigal, Alexis C. "The Man Who Created GPS." *The Atlantic*, June 16, 2014. https://www.theatlantic.com/technology/archive/2014/06/the-man-who-created-gps/372846/.

Mohdin, Aamna. "Gladys West: The Hidden Figure Who Helped Invent GPS." *The Guardian*, November 19, 2020. https://www.theguardian.com/society/2020/nov/19/gladys-west-the-hidden-figure-who-helped-invent-gps.

TPi Zone. "Hidden Figure Gladys West." YouTube, August 11, 2019. https://www.youtube.com/watch?v=Dg4_mqHXtfw.

U.S. Navy. "Navy Hidden Hero: Gladys Mae West and GPS." YouTube, December 19, 2018. https://www.youtube.com/watch?v=McIemoQWv64.



## That's One Small Step for Man, One Giant Leap for Womankind

**The Harvard Computers**

Evans, Claire L. *Broad Band: The Untold Story of the Women Who Made the Internet*. Portfolio, 2018.

Fabbiano, Giuseppina. "The Woman Who Explained the Stars." Review of *What Stars Are Made Of: The Life of Cecilia Payne-Gaposchkin*, by Donovan Moore. *Nature* 578 (February 24, 2020): 509–510. https://www.nature.com/articles/d41586-020-00509-3.

Geiling, Natasha. "The Women Who Mapped the Universe and Still Couldn't Get Any Respect." *Smithsonian Magazine*, September 18, 2013. https://www.smithsonianmag.com/history/the-women-who-mapped-the-universe-and-still-couldnt-get-any-respect-9287444/.

Hirshfeld, Alan. "Williamina Fleming: Brief Life of a Spectrographic Pioneer: 1857–1911." *Harvard Magazine*, January–February 2017. https://www.harvardmagazine.com/2017/01/williamina-fleming.

Sobel, Dava. *The Glass Universe: How the Ladies of the Harvard Observatory Took the Measure of the Stars*. Viking Penguin, 2016.

Williams, Talithia, PhD. *Power in Numbers: The Rebel Women of Mathematics*. Race Point Publishing, 2018.

**Mileva Marić (1875–1948)**

Esterson, Allen, et al. "Women in Science: Struggle & Success, the Tale of Mileva Einstein-Marić, Einstein's Wife." *MIT Press*, March 14, 2019. https://mitpress.mit.edu/blog/women-in-science-struggle-success-the-tale-of-mileva-einstein-maric-einsteins-wife/.

Gagnon, Pauline. "The Forgotten Life of Einstein's First Wife." *Guest Blog. Scientific American*, December 19, 2016. https://blogs.scientificamerican.com/guest-blog/the-forgotten-life-of-einsteins-first-wife/.

Hacker, Kirsten. "Did Albert Einstein Steal the Work on Relativity from His Wife?" (PDF). https://www.eps.mcgill.ca/~courses/c201_winter/Mileva-Maric-Einstein.pdf.

Smith, Dinitia. "Dark Side of Einstein Emerges in His Letters." *New York Times*, November 6, 1996. https://www.nytimes.com/1996/11/06/arts/dark-side-of-einstein-emerges-in-his-letters.html.

Troemel-Ploetz, Senta. "Mileva Einstein-Marić: The Woman Who Did Einstein's Mathematics." *Women's Studies Int. Forum* 13, no. 5 (1990): 415–432. https://236c359f-23d4-4d3a-bf6e-44d9e4d7cc75.filesusr.com/ugd/13fbac_a0a29f94832f4674b-b1c1f1aa0b7e45c.pdf.

Willa-e-Ali. "Mileva Maric—A Forgotten Genius." *Spectra Magazine*, July 21, 2020. https://spectramagazine.org/biography/mileva-maric-a-forgotten-genius/.

Zackheim, Michele. "A Genius Obscured by a Great Man." *Los Angeles Times*, November 14, 1999. https://www.latimes.com/archives/la-xpm-1999-nov-14-op-33310-story.html.

**Katherine Johnson**

Brody, Richard. "'Hidden Figures' is a Subtle and Powerful Work of Counter-History." *New Yorker*, December 23, 2016. https://www.newyorker.com/culture/richard-brody/hidden-figures-is-a-subtle-and-powerful-work-of-counter-history.

Evans, Claire L. *Broad Band: The Untold Story of the Women Who Made the Internet*. Portfolio, 2018.

Fox, Margalit. "Katherine Johnson Dies at 101; Mathematician Broke Barriers at NASA." *New York Times*, Updated July 9, 2020. https://www.nytimes.com/2020/02/24/science/katherine-johnson-dead.html.

Howell, Elizabeth. "The Story of NASA's Real 'Hidden Figures.'" *Scientific American*, January 24, 2017. https://www.scientificamerican.com/article/the-story-of-nasas-real-ldquo-hidden-figures-rdquo/.

Salam, Maya. "Five Women Who Made the Moon Landing Possible." In Her Words, *New York Times*, July 23, 2019. https://www.nytimes.com/2019/07/23/science/moon-landing-women-apollo-11.html.

Shetterly, Margot Lee. "Katherine Johnson Biography." NASA, Updated February 24, 2020. https://www.nasa.gov/content/katherine-johnson-biography.

**Vera Rubin**

Bahcall, Neta A. "Vera Rubin (1928–2016)." *Nature* 542, no. 32 (February 2, 2017). https://www.nature.com/articles/542032a.

Faber, Sandra. "Vera Rubin's Contributions to Astronomy." *Guest Blog. Scientific American*, December 29, 2016. https://blogs.scientificamerican.com/guest-blog/vera-rubins-contributions-to-astronomy/.

Rubin, Vera. "Astronomer Vera Rubin—The Doyenne of Dark Matter." Interview by Josie Glausiusz. *Discover*. https://www.discovermagazine.com/the-sciences/astronomer-vera-rubinthe-doyenne-of-dark-matter.

Rubin, Vera. "Vera Rubin." Interview by Alan Lightman. AIP, April 3, 1989. https://www.aip.org/history-programs/niels-bohr-library/oral-histories/33963.

**Jocelyn Bell Burnell**

Burnell, Jocelyn Bell. "Jocelyn Bell Burnell Reveals the Motivations Behind Her New $3m Graduate-Student Fund." Interview by Matin Durrani. *Diversity and Inclusion. PhysicsWorld*, March 19, 2019. https://physicsworld.com/a/jocelyn-bell-burnell-reveals-the-motivations-behind-her-new-3m-graduate-student-fund/.

Durrani, Matin. "Overlooked for the Nobel: Jocelyn Bell Burnell." *Astronomy and Space* (blog). *PhysicsWorld*, September 30, 2020. https://physicsworld.com/a/overlooked-for-the-nobel-jocelyn-bell-burnell/.

Proudfoot, Ben. "She Changed Astronomy Forever. He Won the Nobel Prize for It." Op-Docs, *New York Times*. https://www.nytimes.com/2021/07/27/opinion/pulsars-jocelyn-bell-burnell-astronomy.html.

## Dropping the Bomb—on Science

**Lise Meitner**

Harris, Margaret. "Overlooked for the Nobel: Lise Meitner." *Nuclear Physics* (blog). *PhysicsWorld*, October 5, 2020. https://physicsworld.com/a/overlooked-for-the-nobel-lise-meitner/.

Sime, Ruth Lewin. *Lise Meitner: A Life in Physics*. University of California Press, 1996.

Sime, Ruth Lewin. "Lise Meitner and the Discovery of Nuclear Fission." *Scientific American*, January 1, 1998. https://www.scientificamerican.com/article/lise-meitner-and-the-discovery-of-n/.

Stille, Darlene R. *Extraordinary Women Scientists*, 138–142. Children's Press, 1995.

**Chien-Shiung Wu**

Hodges, Kate. *I Know a Woman: The Inspiring Connections Between the Women Who Have Shaped Our World.* Aurum Press, 2018.

Johnston, Hamish. "Overlooked for the Nobel: Chien-Shiung Wu." *Particle and Nuclear* (blog). *Physics World*, October 20, 2020. https://physicsworld.com/a/overlooked-for-the-nobel-chien-shiung-wu/.

National Park Service. "Dr. Chien-Shiung Wu, The First Lady of Physics." https://www.nps.gov/people/dr-chien-shiung-wu-the-first-lady-of-physics.htm.

Scutts, Joanna. "The Manhattan Project Physicist Who Fought for Equal Rights for Women." Unsung Women, *Time*, June 14, 2016. https://time.com/4366137/chien-shiung-wu-history/.

Stille, Darlene R., *Extraordinary Women Scientists*, 188–191. Children's Press, 1995.

Weinstock, Maia. "Channeling Ada Lovelace: Chien-Shiung Wu, Courageous Hero of Physics." *Guest Blog. Scientific American*, October 15, 2013. https://blogs.scientificamerican.com/guest-blog/channeling-ada-lovelace-chien-shiung-wu-courageous-hero-of-physics/.

Yuan, Jada. "Discovering Dr. Wu." *Washington Post*, December 13, 2021. https://www.washingtonpost.com/lifestyle/2021/12/13/chien-shiung-wu-biography-physics-grandmother/.

## Women Don't Just Give Life: They Save It

**Trota of Salerno**

Benton, John F. "Trotula, Women's Problems, and the Professionalization of Medicine in the Middle Ages." California Institute of Technology (Revised, November 1984). https://authors.library.caltech.edu/16446/1/HumsWP-0098.pdf.

Benton, John F. "Trotula, Women's Problems, and the Professionalization of Medicine in the Middle Ages." *Bulletin of the History of Medicine* 59, no. 1 (Spring 1985): 30–53. http://www.jstor.org/stable/44452036.

Brooklyn Museum. "Trotula." https://www.brooklynmuseum.org/eascfa/dinner_party/place_settings/trotula.

Drife, J. "The Start of Life: A History of Obstetrics." *Postgraduate Medical Journal* 78, no. 919 (May 2002): 311–315. https://pmj.bmj.com/content/78/919/311#ref-2.

Rowland, Beryl. *Exhuming Trotula*, Sampiens Materna *of Salerno. Florilegium* 1 (1979): 42–57. https://www.utpjournals.press/doi/pdf/10.3138/flor.1.004.

**Mary Hunt**

Bernard, Diane. "How a Miracle Drug Changed the Fight Against Infection During World War II." *Washington Post*, July 11, 2020. https://www.washingtonpost.com/history/2020/07/11/penicillin-coronavirus-florey-wwii-infection/.

Lax, Eric. *The Mold in Dr. Florey's Coat: The Story of the Penicillin Miracle.* Henry Holt, 2004.

Science History Institute. "Howard Walter Florey and Ernst Boris Chain." Updated, December 4, 2017. https://www.sciencehistory.org/historical-profile/howard-walter-florey-and-ernst-boris-chain.

**Elizabeth Bugie Gregory**

ACS. "Selman Waksman and Antibiotics." https://www.acs.org/content/acs/en/education/whatischemistry/landmarks/selmanwaksman.html.

Douglas E. Eveleigh, and Joan W. Bennett. "Women Microbiologists at Rutgers in the Early Golden Age of Antibiotics." In *Women in Microbiology*, 317–329. Edited by Rachel J. Whitaker and Hazel A. Barton. Herndon, VA: American Society for Microbiology Press, 2018.

Google. "Streptomycin and Process of Preparation." Patents. https://patents.google.com/patent/US2449866A/en.

**Esther Lederberg**

Baker, Mitzi. "Esther Lederberg, Pioneer in Genetics, Dies at 83." *Stanford News*, November 29, 2006. https://news.stanford.edu/news/2006/november29/med-esther-112906.html.

Douglas E. Eveleigh, and Joan W. Bennett. "Women Microbiologists at Rutgers in the Early Golden Age of Antibiotics." In *Women in Microbiology*, 317–329. Edited by Rachel J. Whitaker and Hazel A. Barton. Herndon, VA: American Society for Microbiology Press, 2018.

"Esther Lederberg." *Notable Women Scientists*, Gale, 2009. *Science in Context.*

Lee, Jane J. "6 Women Scientists Who Were Snubbed Due to Sexism." *National Geographic*, May 19, 2013. https://www.nationalgeographic.com/culture/article/130519-women-scientists-overlooked-dna-history-science?loggedin=true.

"Microbiology Pioneer." *Stanford Magazine*, March/April 2007. https://stanfordmag.org/contents/microbiology-pioneer.

Schindler, Thomas E. *A Hidden Legacy: The Life and Work of Esther Zimmer Lederberg.* Oxford University Press, 2021.

## It Runs in the Family

**Nettie Stevens**

Brush, Stephen G. "Nettie M. Stevens and the Discovery of Sex Determination by Chromosomes." *Isis* 69, no. 2 (June 1978): 162–72. http://www.jstor.org/stable/230427.

"Nettie Maria Stevens: Celebrating the Work of a Remarkable Geneticist." *History Shapes Our Future* (blog). The Women in Medicine Legacy Foundation, October 5, 2021. https://www.wimlf.org/blog/nettie-maria-stevens-celebrating-the-work-of-a-remarkable-geneticist.

Scitable. "Nettie Stevens: A Discoverer of Sex Chromosomes." https://www.nature.com/scitable/topicpage/nettie-stevens-a-discoverer-of-sex-chromosomes-6580266/.

Smith, Kaitlin. "Nettie Maria Stevens (1861–1912)." *Embryo Project Encyclopedia*, June 20, 2010. https://embryo.asu.edu/pages/nettie-maria-stevens-1861-1912.

Wiley Online Library. "Y Does It Work This Way? Nettie Maria Stevens (July 7, 1861–May 4, 1912). (PDF). https://onlinelibrary.wiley.com/doi/pdf/10.1002/mrd.21390?__cf_chl_jschl_tk__=J_CdjRxFUahgtWX07i-2YTW7USzwu9apflFYe3on-Q_3I-1642055648-0-gaNycG-zNB6U.

**Rosalind Franklin**

Couric, Katie. "1953: Rosalind Franklin." 100 Women of the Year, *Time*, March 5, 2020. https://time.com/5793551/rosalind-franklin-100-women-of-the-year/.

Grady, Denise. "A Revolution at 50; 50 Years Later, Rosalind Franklin's X-Ray Fuels Debate." A Revolution at 50, *New York Times*, February 25, 2003. https://www.nytimes.com/2003/02/25/science/a-revolution-at-50-50-years-later-rosalind-franklin-s-x-ray-fuels-debate.html.

Holt, Jim. "Photo Finish: Rosalind Franklin and the Great DNA Race." *New Yorker*, October 20, 2002. https://www.newyorker.com/magazine/2002/10/28/photo-finish-2.

Lee, Jane J. "Six Women Scientists Who Were Snubbed Due to Sexism." National Geographic, May 19, 2013. https://www.nationalgeographic.com/culture/article/130519-women-scientists-overlooked-dna-history-science?loggedin=true.

Lloyd, Robin. "Rosalind Franklin and DNA: How Wronged Was She?" *Observations* (blog). *Scientific American*, November 3, 2010. https://blogs.scientificamerican.com/observations/rosalind-franklin-and-dna-how-wronged-was-she/.

Maddox, Brenda. *Rosalind Franklin: The Dark Lady of DNA.* HarperCollins, 2002.

Markel, Howard. *The Secret of Life: Rosalind Franklin, James Watson, Francis Crick, and the Discovery of DNA's Double Helix.* W. W. Norton, 2021.

"Rosalind Franklin Was So Much More than the 'Wronged Heroine' of DNA." *Nature*, July 21, 2020. https://www.nature.com/articles/d41586-020-02144-4.

Shapely, Deborah. "Rosalind Franklin and DNA." *New York Times*, September 21, 1975. https://www.nytimes.com/1975/09/21/archives/rosalind-franklin-and-dna.html.

Scitable. "Rosalind Franklin: A Crucial Contribution." https://www.nature.com/scitable/topicpage/rosalind-franklin-a-crucial-contribution-6538012/.

**Marthe Gautier**

Casassus, Barabara. "Down's Syndrome Discovery Dispute Resurfaces in France." *Nature*, February 11, 2014. https://www.nature.com/articles/nature.2014.14690.

Gautier, Marthe. "Fiftieth Anniversary of Trisomy 21: Returning to a Discovery." Translation and Commentary by Peter S. Harper. *Human Genetics* 126 (June 30, 2009): 317–324. https://www.hopkinsmedicine.org/women_science_medicine/_pdfs/trisomy%2021%20article.pdf.

OpenMind. "Great Women Scientists Left in the Shade." Science, Leading Figures, May 11 2015. https://www.bbvaopenmind.com/en/science/leading-figures/great-women-left-in-the-shade-of-science-history/.

Pain, Elisabeth. "After More Than 50 Years, a Dispute Over Down Syndrome Discovery." News, *Science*, February 11, 2014. https://www.science.org/content/article/after-more-50-years-dispute-over-down-syndrome-discovery.

## Coding New Realities

**Ada Lovelace**

Essinger, James. *A Female Genius: How Ada Lovelace, Lord Byron's Daughter, Started the Computer Age*. Gibson Square, 2013.

Evans, Claire L. *Broad Band: The Untold Story of the Women Who Made the Internet*. Portfolio, 2018.

Miller, Claire Cain. "Overlooked: Ada Lovelace." New York Times, https://www.nytimes.com/interactive/2018/obituaries/overlooked-ada-lovelace.html.

**The ENIAC Programmers: Kathleen McNulty, Betty Jean Jennings, Elizabeth Snyder, Marlyn Wescoff, Frances Bilas, and Ruth Lichterman**

Evans, Claire L. *Broad Band: The Untold Story of the Women Who Made the Internet*. Portfolio, 2018.

Penn Engineering. "Celebrating Penn Engineering History: ENIAC." https://www.seas.upenn.edu/about/history-heritage/eniac/.

Porchlight. "Claire Evans Tells the Story of the Computer, and the Internet, through Women Who Developed the Languages They Speak." *Editor's Choice* (blog), March 9, 2018. https://www.porchlightbooks.com/blog/editors-choice/broad-band-the-untold-story-of-the-women-who-made-the-internet.

**Hedy Lamarr**

Dean, Alexandra, dir. *Bombshell: The Hedy Lamarr Story*. Zeitgeist Films, 2017. DCP, Blu-ray, and DVD. https://www.vanityfair.com/hollywood/2017/04/hedy-lamarr-documentary-clip.

Hodges, Kate. *I Know a Woman: The Inspiring Connections Between the Women Who Have Shaped Our World*. Aurum Press, 2018.

Jewell, Hannah. *She Caused a Riot: 100 Women Who Built Cities, Sparked Revolutions, and Massively Crushed It*. Sourcebooks, 2018.

## Who Runs the World? Women.

**Fatima al-Fihri**

Aslan, Reza. *No god but God: The Origins, Evolution, and Future of Islam*. Random House, 2011.

Bellaigue, Christopher de. *The Islamic Enlightenment: The Modern Struggle Between Faith and Reason*. Vintage, 2017.

Bert F. Breiner, and Christian W. Troll, "Christianity and Islam." In *The Oxford Encyclopedia of the Islamic World*. Edited by John L. Esposito. Oxford University Press, 2009.

Errazzouki, Samia. "Morocco: One of the World's Oldest Libraries is Renovated," *AP News*, April 19 2016. https://apnews.com/article/8f07a519e7cd48b58e33bd1babdced40.

Feingold, Mordechai. *History of Universities: Volume XXIV/1&2*. Oxford University Press, 2010.

Landau, Rom. *Morocco: Marrakesh, Fez, Rabat*. Illustrated by Wim Swann. G. P. Putnam's Sons, 1967.

Lewis, David Levering. *God's Crucible: Islam and the Making of Europe, 570–1215*. W. W. Norton, 2008.

Robinson, Jane. *Bluestockings: The Remarkable Story of the First Women to Fight for an Education*. Viking, 2009.

Saini, Angela. *Inferior: How Science Got Women Wrong—and the New Research That's Rewriting the Story*. Boston: Beacon Press, 2017.

Siddiqui, Rafiuddin. "Oldest Library of University of Al-Qarawiyyin in Fez, Morocco." *Pakistan Library & Information Science Journal* 49, no. 3 (July–September 2018): 69–73.

TeachMideast. "Introduction to Women and Gender Roles in the Middle East." http://teachmideast.org/articles/introduction-women-gender-roles-middle-east/.

UNESCO. "More Than One-Half of Children and Adolescents Are Not Learning Worldwide." http://uis.unesco.org/sites/default/files/documents/fs46-more-than-half-children-not-learning-en-2017.pdf.

UNESCO. *The World's Heritage: A Guide to All 981 UNESCO World Heritage Sites*. Collins, 2014.

**Wu Zhao Zetian**

Dash, Mike. "The Demonization of Empress Wu." *Smithsonian Magazine*, August 10, 2012. https://www.smithsonianmag.com/history/the-demonization-of-empress-wu-20743091/.

Deason, Rachel. "The 12 Most Badass Women in Chinese History." Culture Trip, March 6, 2018. https://theculturetrip.com/asia/china/articles/the-12-most-badass-women-in-chinese-history/.

Foreman, Amanda, Dr. "Separation." Episode 2. *The Ascent of Woman*. Directed by Hugo Macgregor, BBC Two, 2015.

Steadman, Ligeia. "Empress Wu." Badass Female Rulers. http://projects.leadr.msu.edu/traditionaleastasia/exhibits/show/badass-female-rulers/empress-wu.

**Martha Matilda Harper**

America's Best Franchises. "Who Was the First Franchisor?" *Franchise Operations* (blog), April 17, 2015. https://americasbestfranchises.com/blog/who-was-the-first-franchisor/.

IFA. "The History of Modern Franchising." *FranBlog*. https://www.franchise.org/blog/the-history-of-modern-franchising.

Parker, Sally. "Martha Matilda Harper and the American Dream." *Rochester Review* 63, no. 1 (Fall 2000). https://www.rochester.edu/pr/Review/V63N1/feature2.html.

Plitt, Jane R. *Martha Matilda Harper and the America Dream: How One Woman Changed the Face of Modern Business*. Syracuse University Press, 2000.

Seaton, Jaimie. "Martha Matilda Harper, the Greatest Businesswoman You've Never Heard Of." Atlas Obscura, January 11, 2017. https://www.atlasobscura.com/articles/martha-matilda-harper-the-greatest-businesswoman-youve-never-heard-of.

# Acknowledgments

*TO HER CREDIT* WOULD NOT HAVE BEEN POSSIBLE WITHOUT THE unwavering support of our agent, Ashley Lopez, at Waxman Literary Agency. Ashley stood by us as the project evolved, guiding us over (many!) years with her expertise and passion.

It is an understatement to say this book would not be what it is without Kezia Gabriella's incredible artwork. Her artwork combines historic references with contemporary, completely original visions, creating imaginative visuals that allow the book to truly come to life.

Kaitlin would like to thank Emily for being a constant inspiration and friend; her sisters for their unconditional love; Clara for always and intuitively understanding; and the friends and family who choose to stay, whose support means the most.

Emily would like to thank Kait for her friendship, dedication to this project, and tireless research; Danya Kukafka for her valuable insights into the world of book publishing; her friends and family around the world who know who they are; and Paul Wiesbrock for always offering his brain as a springboard and, most importantly, for his unconditional support and love.

# Index